DATE DUE

84083			

DEMCO NO. 38-298

FEB 1 1984

New Technology and Documents Librarianship

PROCEEDINGS OF
THE THIRD ANNUAL
LIBRARY GOVERNMENT DOCUMENTS
AND INFORMATION CONFERENCE

ALSO IN THIS SERIES

Collection Development and Public Access
of Government Documents
*Proceedings of the First Annual Library Government
Documents and Information Conference*

Communicating Public Access to Government Information
*Proceedings of the Second Annual Library Government
Documents and Information Conference*

New Technology and Documents Librarianship

PROCEEDINGS OF
THE THIRD ANNUAL
LIBRARY GOVERNMENT DOCUMENTS
AND INFORMATION CONFERENCE

Edited by **Peter Hernon**
Graduate School of Library and
Information Science
Simmons College, Boston

MECKLER PUBLISHING
520 Riverside Avenue, Westport, CT 06880
3 Henrietta Street, London WC2E 8LU, England

Library of Congress Cataloging in Publication Data

Government Documents and Information Conference
     (3rd : 1982 : Columbus, Ohio)
     New technology and documents librarianship.

     Held in Columbus, Ohio, Oct. 1982, sponsored by
Meckler Communications of Westport, Connecticut.
     Bibliography: p.
     1. Libraries–Special collections–Government
publications–Congresses. 2. Libraries, Depository–
United States–Automation–Congresses. 3. United States–
Government publications–Congresses. 4. Government
information–United States–Congresses. 5. Information
storage and retrieval systems–Government publications–
Congresses. I. Hernon, Peter. II. Meckler Communications
(Firm) III. Title.
Z688.G6G66 1982   025.3′434′02854   83-896
ISBN 0-930466-64-0

Printed and bound in the United States of America

CONTENTS

TABLES

FIGURES

PREFACE

The six articles in this book are based on presentations delivered at the Third Annual Library Government Documents and Information Conference sponsored by Meckler Communications of Westport, Connecticut, and held in Columbus, Ohio, in October 1982. The purpose of the conference was to provide an opportunity for writers in the documents field to interact with practicing librarians, library educators, government officials, publishers, library science students, and others interested in a variety of topics relating to government publications/information. In addition, the conference offered a forum for extended discussions of major issues—in this case, new technology and its implications for the development, organization, and servicing of documents collections.

Written by librarians and library educators, the articles examine various aspects of the topic, describe examples of in-house use, identify related trends and issues, and note the application of new technology to decision making and the development of management information systems. They focus not only on the present but also the foreseeable future in order to assist documents librarians in better exploiting available technology, obtaining management information for improved decision making, and increasing access to government information resources.

Governments are extensive producers of information, not all of which appears in print format. Further, a number of libraries are attempting to enhance bibliographic control for nonprint information resources (e.g., audiovisual, map, and machine-readable) and to improve collection organization and the retrieval of the information in the collection. It would seem that new technology (encompassing areas such as micrographics, the role of bibliographic utilities, computerized information systems, in-house retrieval systems, and bibliographic, numeric, and full-text databases) has great potential for documents librarianship of the 1980s and beyond. More information is becoming available in nonbook format; microfiche, for example, has become the primary format in which Government Printing Office depository publications are distributed.[1] Libraries will undoubtedly have to exploit new technology more fully if they want to mediate the information environment and assist their clientele in finding needed information.

This collection of articles complements the proceedings of the second documents conference[2] and a recent issue of *Government Publications Review* (vol. 9, no. 4, 1982) devoted to new technology for the documents field. Together with those two sources, these proceedings explore diverse applications of new technology and chart its present and potential impact on the bibliographic control and availability of government information to library clientele.

In the first article, Charles R. McClure reviews the current uses of micrographics, online bibliographic database searching, computerized information systems, and OCLC in government documents collections. He shows how these technologies can be used for decision making, while pointing out the factors that encourage or retard the utilization of technology. He also makes specific recommendations that will assist documents librarians more effectively to utilize available technology to meet the goals and objectives of their institutions.

Technology can make an impact on access to United States government information in two ways: (1) improved bibliographic access, with catalog records appearing in national databases, and (2) a decrease in published government information, with agencies turning more to computer files and other means of maintaining data for their own use. Judy Myers finds that in both of these areas relevant technology is available and at least partially applied. Outstanding issues relate to the use of this technology—the quality, quantity, timeliness, availability of cataloging data, and the conditions under which government information in nonprint form will be made available to the public. She also focuses on the areas in which decisions are needed and the role of librarians in the national decision-making process.

Bruce Morton discusses various factors that inhibit documents librarians from effectively utilizing computer technology. He stresses that, in the context of collection goals and objectives, there needs to be a raising of administrative consciousness and the development of planning and management skills. He concludes, among other things, that the very large depositories frequently show the most interest in computerizing elements of their operations. Small to medium-sized selective depositories are less likely to have the means or inclination to make use of computer technology, but would nonetheless benefit from computerization.

Commercial online database systems cover government documents to varying degrees. In addition, home delivery information systems can be viewed as a method of disseminating information generated by government agencies and departments to the population in general. However, Susanna Schweizer notes that, at present, few plans exist for any projected or ongoing videotext system to make federal government documents available. Because of this finding, she questions whether federal government documents are suited for the current state-of-the-art home delivery information system.

Terry L. Weech views new technology and state government information resources from two perspectives: (1) the impact of technology on traditional formats of government information services; and (2) the role of technology in the development of new formats for government information. He considers the role of new technology in developing new formats for state government information (e.g., online legislative information systems and video recording of legislative and judicial proceedings) from the perspective of generating new information and improving dissemination and access to information in either new or traditional formats. Information professionals working with both traditional and new formats of state government information must maintain a commitment to public access to such information. In this regard, Weech proposes a new government information professional, one who will ensure that the public's right to know is protected and that state government information is effectively recorded, preserved, and retrieved.

Virginia Gillham discusses CODOC, a computer-based system for processing government documents, which was developed at the University of Guelph in the 1960s. The system enables libraries with sophisticated computer facilities to input and retrieve documents online and in-house. The original batch version of the system, however, can be used at libraries with no on-site computer facilities. In a library, the system provides catalog-type access from six points, including enriched key word, to each individual title in the collection. She also notes that iNET Gateway™, an "intelligent" network developed by the Computer Communications Group of the Trans Canada Telephone System, offers access to an array of information banks. Gillham discusses the significance of the fact that CODOC records are entered in one of these information banks.

Although the articles were written from different perspectives, they nonetheless reveal interrelationships. For example, one theme relates to the value of management information systems and how technology enables libraries to gather the data necessary for improved decision making. Libraries can also develop in-house systems and/or tie into already established systems. The articles remind us that we must all work together to ensure that libraries apply new technology and reap the benefits of it (while minimizing the liabilities).

Libraries can exploit government information while more effectively integrating government publications with other information resources. Use of government publications housed in libraries should increase, in part, once reference staff members and library clientele concentrate on information content and disregard the distinction between formats in which information appears and the level of government producing the information. After all, library clientele want information and often are not concerned about its format. Even if libraries do not adopt the CODOC system, they are reminded that there is at least one system that enriches access to information content and downplays format, issuing agency, and the level of government producing the information.

It is my hope that the literature of documents librarianship benefits from efforts to grapple with major issues and bring together a diversity of informed opinions. It is helpful to understand complex issues and the basic beliefs of authors well known for their contributions to the area of government publications and new technology.

Peter Hernon
Simmons College, Boston
November 1982

References

1. Peter Hernon, "Documents Librarianship in the 1980s: Current Issues and Trends in Research," *Government Publications Review* 9 (1982): 99–120.

2. Peter Hernon, ed., *Communicating Public Access to Government Information. Proceedings of the Second Annual Library Government Documents and Information Conference* (Westport, CT: Meckler Publishing, 1983).

EXPLOITING TECHNOLOGY FOR GOVERNMENT DOCUMENT DEPOSITORY COLLECTIONS: OVERVIEW AND STRATEGIES*

By Charles R. McClure

These are, indeed, challenging times for government document librarians. As this chapter was written, significant changes were occurring in the organization and staffing of the Government Printing Office (GPO). The amount and format of government publishing has been carefully reviewed by the federal government, and policy changes have been offered that will further reduce the amount of information it publishes. Further, many documents collections are facing budget stagnation or outright reductions. The proliferation of information handling technologies appears to offer significant means to reduce costs and increase access to government publications, and document librarians have been presented with unique opportunities to exploit them as a means of increasing the overall effectiveness and efficiency of depository collections.

In recent years, librarians have become accustomed to such phrases as the "information society," "computer revolution," "microprocessors,"

*Portions of this chapter originally appeared in "Technology in Government Document Collections: Current Status, Impacts, and Prospects," *Government Publications Review* 9 (1982): 255–276.

"automated information systems,"˙and many other similar terms. These phrases all assume a fundamental and significant change in the creation, dissemination, and organization of information from that usually considered as "typical" for today's libraries and information centers. The underlying assumption is that applications of information-related technology can (and will) improve the librarian's ability to acquire, organize, and disseminate information. But the impact of recent information-related technology on government documents collections has not received much attention—except in asides relating to library technology in general.

The term "technology" itself is ambiguous, given the breadth of the definitions ascribed to it: applied science, science of mechanical and industrial arts, practices or techniques that improve the human condition, and so forth. But the sense of the word, when considered in the context of libraries and information processing, suggests a less global view: the application of mechanical tools (or their conceptual underpinnings) for improved access, organization and dissemination of information. This definition stresses the importance of technology to the service goals of libraries and the information needs of their users.

The application of technology to government document collections has not been widely discussed, evaluated, or even identified. Without such an assessment, we can easily slip into the traditional dichotomy of viewpoints: technology as panacea versus technology as doom-bringer for society. Both viewpoints ignore the realities confronting government documents librarians who are attempting to make the transition from a traditional mode of library operation to one that exploits those aspects of technology which are *best suited* for a particular library environment.

The purpose of this chapter is to describe the need for document librarians to exploit better the various information handling technologies for depository collections. After some background information about the currently limited access to government publications, this chapter will provide a brief overview of technological applications in the areas of (1) OCLC, (2) online bibliographic database searching, (3) microforms, (4) automated systems, and (5) decision support systems. The chapter will conclude with specific recommendations by which depository documents librarians can better exploit information technologies for integrating access to documents with other types of library materials.

No attempt is made here to review the broad topic of the application of information handling technology in libraries. This information can be obtained by reviewing publications such as the *Annual Review of Information Science and Technology*,[1] appropriate sections of *Library Technology Reports*,[2] *Computer Science Resources*,[3] and journals such as *Information Technology and Libraries*,[4] *Advanced Technology/Libraries*,[5] *Computer*

Equipment Review,[6] and a number of recent publications from Knowledge Industry Publications, Inc., related to applications of library technology.[7] A pragmatic orientation is suggested here to assist the practicing depository librarian to confront the myriad opportunities and constraints related to exploiting technology applications for increased access to government publications.

Technology as a Means to Increase Access and Integration

Numerous reasons can be adduced to justify greater use of information handling technologies in depository collections. Reduced costs for routine chores, better bibliographic control of individual documents, improved user services, and increased cooperation and resource sharing are but some of the reasons typically put forth. While these and other traditional arguments are likely to be true, the primary justification for exploiting technology in depositories is that it will better integrate the depository collections into the library collection as a whole and improve overall access to government publications.

Clearly, the primary problems that limit the utility of government documents tend to have integration and access as common denominators. Integration can be defined as the degree to which bibliographic accessibility, physical availability, professional service, and status of the depository collection match that provided for other materials in the library.[8] Access can be considered in terms of physical, bibliographic, or psychological access to specific information resources printed by the federal government. This concept of integration and access is specified in greater detail in Figure 1-1.

A review of recent research and scholarly writing on access of federal government publications does not evoke optimism. In general terms, the literature (as suggested in Figure 1-2) shows that, comparatively, depository collections receive less funding and fewer resources than other areas in the library; are typically under-utilized; fail to provide adequate reference services—at least in terms of the accuracy of answers provided; are poorly publicized; are not integrated into the library as a whole; are excluded from a number of traditional indexes; operate within a depository library program that lacks meaningful goals, objectives, performance measures and inspection controls; and have only limited bibliographic finding aids and in-house access points.[9]

Yet, despite the various findings listed in Figure 1-2, the current changing federal policy regarding government publications, and the various difficulties encountered by depository libraries in providing adequate integration and access to government information, a recent

Figure 1-1: The Concept of Integration

CRITERIA	INDICATORS
1. BIBLIOGRAPHIC ACCESSIBILITY	Does the patron have the same probability of determining the existence of a certain government publication as he does of determining the existence of an information source of a more traditional format? Does the patron have equal access to indexes and reference tools related to government publications as to those related to other information sources in the library? Does the patron have the same probability of obtaining specific information within the government publication as he does with an information source in a more traditional format?
2. PHYSICAL AVAILABILITY	Does the patron have the same probability of locating and obtaining a specific government document (once its existence within the library is verified) as of any other type of material in the library? Does the patron have the same opportunity to locate and obtain government publications regardless of format, i.e., microforms, maps, and A-V?
3. PROFESSIONAL SERVICE	Does the patron have the same awareness of the information sources available in government publications as for other information sources in a more traditional format? Does the patron have the same opportunity to be referred to an appropriate government publication as for other information sources in the library? Does the patron deal with librarians who are as competent, trained, and knowledgeable about government publications as librarians with other competencies, training, and knowledge related to their specific areas of responsibility?
4. STATUS	Do government documents receive similar resource support (staff, materials, equipment, etc.) as do other areas/departments in the library? Do the document librarians participate in library administrative matters to the same extent as other librarians? Do the director and librarians perceive government publications to be as valuable an information resource as other library information resources?

**Figure 1-2: Summary of Selected, Recent Research
and Writings (1978 to mid-1982) on Access of
Government Publications in Depository Collections**

Author(s)	Date	Findings
Cook[a]	1981	Minimal staffing, reduced budget, and fewer resources for documents departments compared to other areas of the library
Fry[b]	1978	Under-utilization and nonrecognition of the value of government publications
Heisser, Palmatier, and McClure[c]	1981	Ineffectiveness of the Depository Library Inspection Program and compliance with "minimum standards" by depository libraries
Hernon[d]	1979	Non-use of government publications by social scientists, and a small minority of documents account for vast majority of all use
Hernon[e]	1982	Depository collections of microformatted government documents either go unused or a small percentage of the collection receives the most use
Hernon and McClure[f]	1982	Depository library staff answered 37% of test questions—reference service not of high quality
Hernon and Purcell[g]	1982	Depositories constitute but one of the information providers to access government information, and oftentimes it is a secondary one. Further, depositories often select more publications than are needed
Hernon and Shepard[h]	1982	The *Social Science Citation Index* contains a minimal number of citations to government publications
Hoduski[i]	1983	Document libraries must publicize and promote documents as well as take political action to effect changes in the depository system or the local library
McClure[j]	1977	Nonintegration of microformatted government documents into the collection as a whole
McClure[k]	1978	Exclusion of many government periodicals from traditional periodical indexes

Figure 1-2: Continued

McClure[l]	1981	Nonintegration of government documents into library administrative, reference, and collection development processes
McClure[m]	1981 & 1982	Inability of documents librarians to exploit new technologies such as on-line database searching, OCLC, and in-house automated systems
McClure[n]	1982	Structural limitations, lack of measurable goals, objectives and meaningful performance measures, and limited evaluation of the effectiveness for the Depository System
McClure and Harman[o]	1982	Limited inclusion of references to government publications in doctoral dissertations
NCLIS[p]	1982	Confusion between the role of the public and private sectors as to responsibilities for acquisition, dissemination, and bibliographic control of government publications
Richardson, et al.[q]	1980	Minimal bibliographic access points and in-house finding aids for documents

Sources
a. Kevin L. Cook, "A Study of Varying Levels of Support Given to Government Documents Collections in Academic Libraries" (Master's thesis, University of Oklahoma, 1981).
b. Bernard M. Fry, *Government Publications: Their Role in the National Program for Libraries and Information Services* (Washington, DC: Government Printing Office, 1978).
c. David C. Heisser, Roxanne Palmatier, and Charles R. McClure, "GPO Inspection Program," *Government Publications Review* 7A (1980): 450–52.
d. Peter Hernon, *Use of Government Publications by Social Scientists* (Norwood, NJ: Ablex Publishing Corp., 1979).
e. _____, *Microforms and Government Information* (Westport, CT: Microform Review, Inc., 1981).
f. Peter Hernon and Charles R. McClure, "Testing the Quality of Reference Services Provided by Academic Depositories: A Pilot Study," in *Communicating Public Access to Government Information*, ed. Peter Hernon (Westport, CT: Meckler Publishing, 1983).

Figure 1-2: Continued

g. Peter Hernon and Gary R. Purcell, *Developing Collections of U.S. Government Publications* (Greenwich, CT: JAI Press, 1982).

h. Peter Hernon and Clayton A. Shepard, "Government Documents in Social Science Literature," in *Collection Development and Public Access of Government Documents*, ed. Peter Hernon (Westport, CT: Meckler Publishing, 1982).

i. Bernadine Hoduski, "Political Activism for Documents Librarians," in *Communicating Public Access to Government Information*, ed. Peter Hernon (Westport, CT: Meckler Publishing, 1983).

j. Charles R. McClure, "Administrative Integration of Microformatted Government Documents," *Microform Review* 6 (September 1977): 259–71.

k. _____, "Indexing U.S. Government Periodicals: Analysis and Comments," *Government Publications Review* 5 (1978): 409–21.

l. _____, "Administrative Basics for Microformatted Government Documents Librarians," in *Microforms and Government Information*, ed. Peter Hernon (Westport, CT: Microform Review, Inc., 1981), 125–45.

m. _____, "Online Government Documents Data Base Searching and the Use of Microfiche Documents Online by Academic and Public Depository Librarians," *Microform Review* 10 (Fall, 1981): 245–59; and idem, "Technology in Government Documents Collections," *Government Publications Review* 9 (1982): 255–76.

n. _____, "Structural Analysis of the Depository System: A Preliminary Assessment," in *Collection Development and Public Access of Government Documents*, ed. Peter Hernon (Westport, CT: Meckler Publishing, 1982), 35–36.

o. Charles R. McClure and Keith Harman, "Government Documents as Bibliographic References and Sources in Dissertations," *Government Publications Review* 9 (1982): 61–72.

p. National Commission on Libraries and Information Science, *Public Sector/Private Sector Interaction in Providing Information Services* (Washington, DC: Government Printing Office, 1982).

q. John V. Richardson, Jr., Dennis C. W. Frisch, and Catherine M. Hall, "Bibliographic Organization of U.S. Federal Depository Collections," *Government Publications Review* 7A (1980): 463–80.

Source: Charles R. McClure and Peter Hernon, *Improving the Quality of Reference Service for Government Publications* (Chicago: American Library Association, 1983).

report from the National Commission on Libraries and Information Science concluded:

The federal government should actively use existing mechanisms, such as the libraries of the country, as primary channels for making governmentally distributable information available to the public.[10]

Thus, it is likely that libraries, especially members of the depository program, will continue to be perceived as playing a significant role in the dissemination of, and access to, government information in the foreseeable future.

Exploiting various information handling technologies appears to be one avenue that depository librarians have yet to maximize as a means to increase integration of, and access to, government publications. Further, in many instances, the various information handling technologies have not as yet been analyzed concerning their specific impacts, costs and benefits for the typical depository collection. One conclusion, however, is clear. Government documents depository librarians generally have failed to integrate documents successfully into overall library services and operations, nor have they significantly increased access to these valuable materials in recent years. To examine this conclusion more closely, a review of some of the currently available information handling technologies with potential applications for the depository library collection is necessary.

OCLC

A very familiar, and recently pervasive, application of technology to libraries and information centers has been OCLC. While originally developed to provide an online union catalog and assist in the cataloging of library materials, subsystems such as serials control, interlibrary loan, and acquisitions have since been added to it. Further, OCLC provides significant applications for public services related to government publications in terms of bibliographic verification and "subject searches" via the Superintendent of Documents Classification search key. But, one must remember that only since July of 1976 has the Government Printing Office (GPO) been inputting publications into OCLC for the preparation of the *Monthly Catalog*.

Although the usefulness of OCLC and the appropriateness of its various subsystems are becoming better known to documents librarians, the degree to which OCLC is actually utilized in depository collections, the specific activities for which it is used, and the availability of OCLC to the depository collection deserve additional attention. Clearly, knowledge of its usefulness and applications is not the same as implementing the technology in the typical depository library setting.

In a survey conducted in 1981 by this writer, a sample of academic and public library depositories responded to questions regarding their use of OCLC.[11] Table 1-1 summarizes the results from that survey in which 77 percent of a 221 sample responded. Although three-quarters of the academic depository libraries and almost half of the public library depository libraries have an OCLC terminal in their library, only 5 percent of those that have separate documents collections have a terminal in the documents area. Furthermore, the number of professional documents librarians, as well as the paraprofessionals with OCLC training, is less than 1 percent. And finally, the average OCLC search time per week by the professional documents librarians is approximately 30 minutes.

These data suggest that limited use and application of OCLC is currently being made by depository librarians. Indeed, with virtually no formal training for documents staff in the use of OCLC, sophisticated use of the system, its subsystem, or individualized applications for a specific depository library collection is not likely. And without OCLC terminals in the documents collections (given that 75 percent of the depositories have separate collections), application of OCLC technology to government publications collections is reduced even further. Although individual examples of OCLC applications can be identified,[12] by and large, significant application of OCLC to government documents collections remains a goal rather than a reality.

Online Bibliographic Database Searching

Access to online bibliographic databases primarily containing government publications has increased significantly since 1978, owing to the number of databases that have been made available through Lockheed DIALOG, Systems Development Corporation's ORBIT, and BRS.[13] Online searching of government document databases can: provide increased access to specific types of government publications not indexed elsewhere; reduce the time lag between availability of the document and its bibliographic access; reduce expenses by eliminating the need to purchase numerous hardcopy indexes that may be only infrequently used; reduce time needed for actual searching; increase search strategies and effectiveness of searches because of Boolean and proximity operators (amongst other techniques); increase access to documents because they have been tagged by search fields unique to government

Table 1-1: Utilization of OCLC by Academic and Public Depository Libraries

	% Academic	% Public
A. Summary Data		
1. Percent with OCLC Terminal in Documents Area	5	5
2. Percent with OCLC Terminal in the Library	75	45
3. Percent of Professional document librarians with OCLC Training	1	1
4. Percent of Paraprofessional documents staff with OCLC Training	.5	.2
5. Number of OCLC search hours per week by professional documents librarians	.5 (Hours)	.4 (Hours)
B. Reasons Given for Use of OCLC (Percent Agreeing*)		
1. Obtain SUDOC number	77	60
2. Obtain Documents Cataloging Information	67	60
3. Verify Interlibrary Loan Bibliographic Data	41	80
4. Request government documents on interlibrary loan	29	40
5. Input Records	14	20
6. Other	20	10
C. Reasons Given for Non-Use of OCLC (Percent Agreeing*)		
1. No OCLC Terminals	33	61
2. Other Librarians do government document searching as needed	50	27
3. The library cannot afford to use OCLC terminals for government publications	10	26
4. Cannot convince library administrators that OCLC is necessary for government publications	6	12
5. Document Librarians/staff do not know how to use OCLC	25	11

*Respondents could check as many reasons as applied to their situation, therefore, columns do not total 100%

Source: Charles R. McClure, "Technology in Government Document Collections: Current Status, Impacts, and Prospects," *Government Publications Review* 9 (1982): 255-76.

publications; and reduce search problems because of controlled vocabulary with various index fields. Further, online searching can assist collection management by utilizing information in the various search fields, such as publication year, format, agency and others. However, difficulties regarding staff training, access to appropriate computer equipment, and online search costs can limit the application of this technology to government documents collections.

A survey conducted by this writer sampled academic and public depository librarians regarding their use of online database searching. This survey, discussed above in the section on OCLC, attempted to identify the amount of online searching being done by documents librarians, the amount of formal training received, the frequency of searching in the specific databases that emphasize government publications, and the reasons for the use or disuse of this technology.

A complete discussion of data from that study cannot be presented in the limited space available here, but summary data of specific interest to this chapter are presented in Tables 1-2 and 1-3. Seven percent or fewer of the depository libraries (those with separate collections) have terminals for online searching in the documents area, although 65 percent of the academic and 35 percent of the public libraries have terminals; 66 percent of the professional documents librarians have received no training on either DIALOG, ORBIT, or BRS; and online search time for documents librarians is approximately 10 minutes per week.

The response that "other librarians do online data base searching" is representative of a growing trend in libraries in which online database searching activities are centralized in one department—typically the reference department. Given the complexities and idiosyncracies of the techniques uniquely required to search government document databases, the effectiveness of searches done by non-documents librarians can be questioned. Nonetheless, data from this study suggest limited involvement by documents librarians in online training sessions. Thus, when searching is to be done, other librarians must do it.

In summary, the survey's findings suggest that limited online database searching is presently being undertaken in academic and public depository libraries. The depositories in public libraries provide substantially fewer online services than do academic depositories. Depositories that tend to provide online services may be characterized as being academic libraries in the western region of the United States, and their librarians are likely to have had formal training on the DIALOG system.

Table 1-2: Summary of Online Activity

	Academic		Public	
1. Percent of depository librarians trained for online searching on either SDC, DIALOG, or BRS	40%		20%	
2. Online Data Base Search hours per week by depository librarians and documents staff	.2		.1	
3. Total number of Online Searches per month by depository librarians and documents staff	3.1		.7	
	% Yes	% No	% Yes	% No
4. Percent of depositories with computer terminals for Online Data Base Searching *in Documents Area* (only those with separate documents area)	7	93	3	97
5. Percent of depositories with computer terminal *in library* for Online Data Base Searching	65	35	35	65
6. Percent of depositories with budgeted amount for Online Data Base Searching	17	83	14	86

Source: Charles R. McClure, "Technology in Government Document Collections: Current Status, Impacts, and Prospects," *Government Publications Review* 9 (1982): 255-76.

Table 1-3: Reasons Given for Why Online Data Base Searching Is Not Done by Depository Librarians

Reason	Percent Agreeing[*]	
	Academic	Public
1. Other librarians do Online Data Base Searching	53%	27%
2. No terminals	35%	60%
3. Online searching of government documents data bases not seen as important by administrators or other librarians	8%	8%
4. No money available	14%	38%
5. Prefer hard copy reference tools	12%	3%
6. Other	21%[**]	3%

[*]Respondents could check more than one reason, therefore columns do not total 100%

[**]Includes 12% of academic respondents who indicated that online data base searching was not "necessary" for the department to provide adequate information services.

Source: Charles R. McClure, "Online Government Documents Data Base Searching and the Use of Microfiche Documents Online by Academic and Public Depository Librarians," *Microform Review* 10 (Fall 1981): 245–59.

13

Microforms

The utilization of microformatted information handling technology can best be described as a love/hate affair for most documents librarians. On the one hand, reduced storage costs, compact shelving benefits and more efficient and less expensive duplication (fiche to fiche) have encouraged the love aspect of the relationship; but the difficulties arising from the organization and bibliographic control of microformatted materials, equipment needs and costs, ever-present complaints about the format's difficulties of use, eyestrain and reduced availability in terms of circulation continue to plague both users and librarians.[14]

In 1976, the Joint Committee on Printing approved microfiche distribution through the depository library program. The first shipments of depository microfiches were distributed in 1977, and guidelines for GPO microfiche conversion have recently been developed.[15] Presently, microformatted government publications can be obtained from numerous non-GPO, U.S. government agencies, a number of state governments, the United Nations, national and international agencies, and a host of commercial publishers. In the near future, the number of microformatted documents available for purchase or through the depository program can be expected to equal, if not surpass, the number of hardcopy documents being published.

With an estimated 35,000 microfiche titles shipped by the GPO to depository libraries in 1982 and the likelihood that the number will increase, the depositories' ability to apply this technology effectively for improved access, organization, and dissemination of government information will take on greater importance in the immediate future. Yet many depositories have inadequate micro-related equipment, including readers, reader-printers, fiche-to-fiche duplicators and storage cabinets.[16] Further, depositories separated from main library collections frequently are forced to "piggyback" their micro-related equipment needs on other departments physically distant from the documents department—which limits rather than increases access to microformatted government documents.[17]

In a related area, microform technology has been recently developed to access microformatted government publications online. Documents librarians can identify and examine an abstract of the document and order a microfiche copy online in minutes. The wedding of online bibliographic database searching technology and microform technology has great potential for increased access to documents—especially with the growing number of databases that offer this service. Yet, in the survey mentioned above conducted by this writer, it was revealed that only 3 percent of the depository libraries have *ever* ordered microfiche

Table 1-4: Microformatted Government Publications Online

A. Use of Online Government Publications in Microform

Variable	Academic		Public	
1. Average number of microfiche ordered online per month	0		0	
2. Percent of depositories that have ever ordered microfiche online	YES 3%	NO 97%	YES 0	NO 100%

B. Reasons Given For Why Government Documents in Microfiche Are Not Ordered Online

	Percent Agreeing*	
Reason	Academic	Public
1. The library does not have computer terminals	33%	59%
2. Didn't know microfiche government documents could be ordered online	24%	25%
3. Prefer hard copy rather than microfiche	27%	20%
4. No money available to purchase microfiche	17%	17%
5. No reason to order microfiche when available free as hardcopy depository item	18%	9%
6. Library already subscribes to ERIC and/or NTIS Microfiche	14%	3%
7. Other	21%	17%

*Respondents could check more than one reason, therefore, columns do not total 100%.

Source: Charles R. McClure, "Online Government Documents Data Base Searching and the Use of Microfiche Documents Online by Academic and Public Depository Librarians," *Microform Review* 10 (Fall 1981): 245-59.

online. The results of the survey are summarized in Table 1-4. Primary reasons given for this disuse include: (1) Computer terminals are not available to the documents librarians; (2) depository librarians are unaware that microfiche could be ordered directly online; and (3) there is a preference for ordering hardcopy documents rather than microfiche whenever possible.

These and other difficulties have made the successful application of microformatted information handling technologies in documents areas most troublesome. A scanning of minutes from recent meetings of the Depository Library Council, of articles and notes appearing in *Documents to the People*, and discussions with depository librarians suggest that there is significant frustration with microform technology. One reason for it, perhaps, is the fact that many depository libraries did not actively *choose* to apply this technology in their libraries; the decision regarding formats, titles, and procedures for distributing and making available microformatted documents came largely from private micropublishers and the federal government. Depository librarians were on the receiving end of a technology on the appropriateness of which they had little to say.

Despite these difficulties, innovative approaches are arising in some depository libraries to utilize and apply microform technology for increased distribution, access, and bibliographic control, rather than for its original function of preservation and storage space reduction.

Automated Systems

For the purposes of this chapter, an automated system will be defined as a computer-based system that accomplishes specific goals related to the access, organization, or dissemination of information in a documents collection, and/or one that provides management information that assists the librarian in making decisions related to the collection. Typically, an automated system can include bibliographic information, textual information, circulation data, acquisitions information, user information and a host of management data, including budgets, personnel records, inventories and more. There are a number of useful sources that can introduce the documents librarian to automated systems and online services.[18]

As applied to government documents collections, automated systems can be developed under any of the following approaches:[19]

- Purchase or lease a turn-key system (i.e., a system "ready to operate")
- Share an automated system with another library via a network or through a formal cooperative agreement
- Modify a system from another library

- Piggyback the system onto already available institutional hardware and software
- Develop the system locally

Although these approaches are presented individually for purposes of illustration, in practice they are often combined as a means of developing the final product.

But, given the constraints typically facing the depository documents collection (i.e., limited staff, resources, and time), documents librarians have only recently initiated the use of automated systems for various document-related activities. A common approach is to utilize OCLC through one or more of its subsystems to develop applications useful specifically for a documents collection. For many depository documents collections, establishing an automated system through OCLC is likely to be the most readily available opportunity to utilize computer technology for improved management and access.

Most depository libraries are not likely, at this time, to have either developed such systems or to be utilizing available computer technology to better manage, control and make available the documents in their collections. Indeed, such systems develop largely out of the personal interest and dedication of one individual. Instances where a local system has been developed and then fails because the one person responsible for it leaves the employ of the institution are not uncommon. At one depository collection, an in-house KWIC-KWOC index program was used as a means to organize, access and control a collection of state publications. The index was a smashing success, but it died when its creator left the institution. Other similar examples demonstrate the widespread failure to train a successor to continue the system, as well as a lack of administrative support.

For most depository collections, automated systems specifically designed for documents collections are a dream rather than a reality. Commercial vendors of automated systems have not invested the start-up capital necessary for turn-key systems specially designed for documents collections. In this writer's view, the most significant development in automated systems application in the documents department is the use of preexisting institutional software packages. In many academic institutions and local governments, numerous software packages are available and being used for various forms of records management. The use of these software programs for documents collections management can be accomplished *without* sophisticated programming skills (since the software is "canned"), without significant cost, but with impressive benefits for accessing the collection. The critical ingredients for success, it appears, are the *desire and dedication* of the documents librarian to attempt the development of the systems!

Decision Support Systems

The administrative environment in depository collections today calls for accurate, timely, insightful, and effective decisions that facilitate the documents librarian's ability to accomplish predetermined goals and objectives. Because of rapidly changing circumstances, the development and use of management information takes on increased importance. Indeed, the complexities of administrating a medium to large academic or public depository library collection require: (1) a conceptual approach by which the library identifies, collects, and presents information for library decision making, and (2) a practical approach by which procedures, techniques, and equipment are coordinated to provide librarians with information for improving the effectiveness and efficiency of the various library services and operations.

The term "decision support systems" (DSS) was introduced relatively recently and has been variously defined in the literature. Heindel and Napier suggest that DSS is "a blending of computer information with decision-making analysis techniques from management science and operations research."[20] Akoka defines it as "a category of information systems used in organizations to assist managers in semi-structured decision processes,"[21] as opposed to the more routine and programmed decision processes. Boomer and Chorba view DSS as a "natural progression from electronic data processing (EDP) and management information systems (MIS) in which information systems are designed to conform to the unique style and needs of a manager so as to assist him/her in determining the solutions to all problems."[22]

Where the typical documents librarian lacks adequate clerical staff—to say nothing of word processing equipment, WATS telephone lines and other automated office niceties—a decision support system may seem to be nothing more than a pipe dream. However, one might suggest that a significant reason for the lack of integration of, and access to, depository documents is the inability of the documents librarian to make informed, accurate, and timely decisions based on empirical evidence rather than "best opinion."[23]

As suggested above, two levels of activities are necessary for the development of a decision support system. First, there is a need for a conceptual foundation on which such a system can be developed. One possible approach is suggested in Figure 1-3. At a more practical level, some thought must be given to the specific data elements appropriate to include in the decision support system. A method to assist the documents librarian in identifying specific data elements is suggested in Figure 1-4.[24] When used together, these two figures may provide the documents librarian with a point of departure for developing a decision support system specifically for depository documents collections.

Figure 1-3: Design Considerations for the Development of a System for Library Management Information

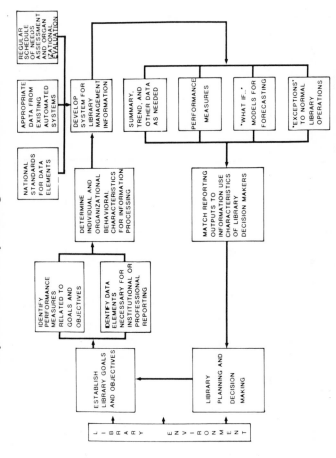

Source: Charles R. McClure, "Management Information for Library Decision Making," in W. Simonton, ed., *Advances in Librarianship*, vol. 12 (New York: Academic Press, 1983).

Figure 1-4: Classification Scheme for Recording and Reporting Information about Libraries

Measures / Programmatic Functions	Financial Measures	Personnel Measures	Facility Measures	Activity Measures	User Measures	Outcome/ Performance Measures
Informational, Educational, Cultural and Recreational Services						
Resource Distribution Services						
Collection Development Serices						
Technical Serices						
Administrative and Support Services						

Source: *Library Data Collection Handbook* (Chicago: American Library Association, 1981), p. 19.

Clearly, the number of decision support systems actually in use in *any* library setting is minimal; thus, one would not be surprised to learn that there is even less chance of such systems being in operation at depository collections. Nonetheless, depository librarians (if they are to increase integration of, and access to, government publications) must attend to the development of systems that provide ongoing, accurate and timely management information about a broad range of depository-related activities. Indeed, support for such ongoing evaluation and assessment of the depository collection is essential for effective services, operations and planning.[25]

Exploiting Technology for Depository Collections

Obtain Training

As the previous section, which surveyed the use of technology in government documents collections, suggests, most documents librarians currently have little training with online bibliographic database searching, OCLC, microcomputers, computer software applications, and little knowledge about computers, programming, video applications, etc. By and large, this constraint is self-imposed and can be removed *only* by a conscious decision on the part of the documents librarian. Until the documents librarian decides to utilize appropriate technology, to better understand potential applications for the documents collection, and to upgrade his or her competence in this area, removal of other constraints is not likely to occur. Yet, of all the strategies to be discussed, this initial decision is the easiest to make, and it is the one over which the documents librarian has the greatest control.

Numerous strategies exist to obtain necessary training. With over two-thirds of the depository libraries in academic institutions (many of which encourage staff to take courses by providing time off or payment of tuition), librarians have access to formal courses related to technology applications. Attending short courses or workshops also can be an efficient means of introducing oneself to a topic of interest. Many automation vendors offer training seminars at reasonable prices. And another approach is to obtain a mentor in the specific technological area of interest. Self-initiated learning oftentimes is more effective than other, more traditional forms of continuing education. Regardless of which approach is taken, the fact remains that documents librarians have many opportunities for training.

Minimize Costs

The first concern typically raised by the documents librarian has to do with the perceived costs associated with the utilization of library technology. One point to be made is that, in many cases, costs can be minimal. For instance, the purchase of a microcomputer with some disk storage capacity can be less than $2,500 (1982 dollars). And the costs can be further reduced if they are shared by the entire library or other agencies/departments within the library. Second, it is likely that the documents department already has access to various technologies *if the librarian were only to ask!*

For instance, many depository collections in universities and colleges could access the university computer system and its software simply by requesting a password from the appropriate people. Public depository libraries have the same potential to access a city/council computer system. In many cases, all one has to do is have a specific and viable use of the system in mind and ask. In short, while outright purchases of most information handling technologies are not feasible for many documents collections, they can often be integrated through existing institutional programs.

In many instances, depository librarians can initiate information handling technologies without any capital outlay. How? In most instances, these services already are supported by the institution for the benefit of the whole. What is required, primarily is the "piggybacking" of the technology for the documents collection onto preexistent systems in the institution or local government.

Set Priorities and Reduce Workload

Numerous surveys indicate that the typical depository collection has one full-time professional and one paraprofessional, with minimal student or volunteer assistance.[26] Thus, documents librarians who are conscientious in meeting the responsibilities of the profession and who attempt to follow the guidelines from the Government Printing Office continually find themselves with too much work and too little staff to get it all done.

At the outset, we can agree that *all* the work and *all* the duties are not likely to be accomplished in the near future, regardless of how hard one works! Thus, it is suggested that the documents librarian must formulate written priorities and objectives for what is (and is not) to be accomplished. In outlining such priorities, it is appropriate—indeed, necessary—to include objectives related to identifying and implementing technological applications. Given these priorities, and with proper discussion with various administrators in the library, some of the *less* important (but not unimportant) activities simply must be put on the back burner.

It is not likely that the documents collections will receive an influx of staff and a reduction in duties in the foreseeable future. Thus, to eschew the possible applications of technology in the documents collection on the basis of workload and limited staff is tantamount to saying that such applications will never be implemented. Finally, it should be stressed that effectively implementing various forms of technology can reduce traditional work responsibilities. Indeed, after initial start-up commitments, many of the technological applications discussed in this chapter are, in themselves, the best means of removing the constraints related to workload and staffing.

Increase Priority for Government Documents
A frequent comment made by documents librarians is that the documents collection receives low priority—relative to other departments or areas in the library (assuming the collection is separate)—when technological applications are considered. Such a situation is a political or administrative constraint, which can only be removed by the documents librarian who demonstrates: (1) the overall importance of the documents collection and the necessity for it to be integrated (philosophically, administratively, and in terms of service) into the library as a whole; (2) a concrete plan of action for how appropriate technologies can be utilized effectively in the collection; and (3) a strategy of technology utilization that "piggy-backs" applications from other systems or otherwise has limited cost.

Low priority may be placed on utilization of technology in the documents areas because of perceived costs, inappropriateness of such technologies for documents, or lack of resultant benefits. The strategy in this case is for the documents librarian to "market" and promote the appropriateness of technology utilization for the collection within the context of library-wide goals and objectives. Such a strategy implies obtaining political support from other library staff and being able to demonstrate clearly the specific benefits that would result from technology utilization. Marketing the usefulness of various technology applications must come *after* the documents librarian has had adequate training and acquired knowledge of the technologies applicable to the collection.

Finally, the documents librarian must be constantly on the lookout for "piggybacking" or other opportunities to involve the collection in the technological applications intended primarily for other areas. Volunteer for online database training, even if the terminals are in the reference department; better to have *some* searching of government documents databases by the documents librarians than *none*! Investigate the use of existing technologies with an eye to applications in the documents department. Oftentimes, a low institutional priority can be overcome by strategic planning, expanding the department's political power base, and "piggybacking" documents use of technological applications onto existing systems either in the library or the institution at large.

Obtain Technology Utilization Information
Obtaining information about information handling technologies as applied to government documents collections is a difficult task. As suggested in the first section of this chapter, there are very few sources that describe the applications of technology specifically to government documents collections. Indeed, searching the traditional library-related indexes for publications about technology applications in government documents collections is an exercise in frustration.

To resolve this difficulty, a number of strategies are necessary. First, documents librarians who have had experience with various types of technological applications should submit written plans, reports, and studies to ERIC for access by other documents librarians. Second, those librarians who have initiated technological applications in the documents collections but have not produced any written summaries of their projects should do so, and make the information available. Finally, the American Library Association's GODORT (Government Documents Round Table) could take on the responsibility of providing clearinghouse information regarding the application of information handling technologies in documents collections.

Challenges for the Future

The survey information and overview presented in this chapter suggest that there is minimal application of various information handling technologies in the areas of OCLC, online bibliographic database searching, automated systems, and decision support systems in depository library settings. However, individual activities and successes can be identified. The following constraints can limit technological applications in government documents collections: complacent documents librarians, training, cost, workload and staffing, low priority of documents, and access to technology utilization information. In each of these areas, the documents librarian can develop strategies to minimize the impact of these constraints.

Training is easily available; the costs of some applications are minimal, especially if they can be "piggybacked" onto other library or institutional applications; excessive workload and limited staffing can be remedied by setting priorities and using the technology as a means of reducing workload; clear demonstration of benefits resulting from technological applications and the importance of materials in the documents collection can raise the presently low priority assigned to documents; and becoming more involved in professional associations and sharing available information about technology applications will allow us to learn from each other. However, the documents librarian must take on this responsibility and provide the initiative for utilizing various information handling technologies in the documents collection.

The challenge to documents librarians to apply technology for increased access to government documents is to rise above the endless daily routines, to escape from preconceived notions about traditional library/information services and the depository library system, and to set priorities as to how the depository collection can best utilize information handling technologies to benefit both the library and the user. Once the priorities are determined, the depository librarian can then *initiate* a program to assess potential applications of technology in his/her library, develop a plan to implement such applications, and go about the business of exploiting specific technologies for increased access, organization, and dissemination of government information. For the time being, the success of technological applications in depository collections will be determined more by the initiative and dedication of the individual documents librarian than by the availability and appropriateness of the technology!

References

1. Martha E. Williams, ed., *Annual Review of Information Science and Technology* (White Plains, NY: Knowledge Industries, annual).

2. *Library Technology Reports* (Chicago: American Library Association, bimonthly).

3. Darlene Myers, ed. and comp., *Computer Science Resources: A Guide to Professional Literature* (White Plains, NY: Knowledge Industries, 1981).

4. *Information Technology and Libraries* (Chicago: American Library Association, quarterly).

5. *Advanced Technology Libraries* (White Plains, NY: Knowledge Industries, monthly).

6. *Computer Equipment Review* (Westport, CT: Meckler Publishing).

7. Knowledge Industry Publications, Inc., White Plains, New York. A catalog of recent publications can be requested.

8. Charles R. McClure, "An Integrated Approach to Government Publication Collection Development," *Government Publications Review* 8A (1981):5–15.

9. Charles R. McClure and Peter Hernon, *Improving the Quality of Reference Service for Government Publications* (Chicago: American Library Association, 1983).

10. National Commission on Libraries and Information Science, *Public Sector/Private Sector Interaction in Providing Information Services* (Washington, DC: Government Printing Office, 1982), p. 52.

11. A description of the survey and its methodology can be found in Charles R. McClure, "Online Government Documents Data Base Searching and the Use of Microfiche Documents Online by Academic and Public Depository Librarians," *Microform Review* 10 (Fall 1981): 246–48.

12. Sharon Walbridge, "OCLC and Government Documents Collections," *Government Publications Review* 9 (1982):277–87.

13. Deborah S. Hunt, "Accessing Federal Government Documents Online," *Database* 6 (1982):10–17; and Linda Futato, "Online Bibliographic Database Searching for Government Documents Collections," *Government Publications Review* 9 (1982):311–22.

14. Stephen R. Salmon, "User Resistance to Microforms in the Research Library," *Microform Review* 3 (July 1974): 194–99.

15. "Guidelines For Microfiche Conversion," *Documents to the People* 9 (September 1981): 218–20.

16. Anne Shaw, "GODORT Microform Survey," *Documents to the People* 6 (January 1978): 27–28.

17. Charles R. McClure, "Microformatted Government Publications: Space and Facilities," *Government Publications Review* 6 (1979); 405–12.

18. *See,* for example: Joseph R. Matthews, *Choosing an Automated Library System: A Planning Guide* (Chicago: ALA, 1980); Richard W. Boss, *The Library Manager's Guide to Automation* (White Plains, NY: Knowledge Industries, 1979); and Ryan E. Hoover, *The Library and Information Manager's Guide to Online Services* (White Plains, NY: Knowledge Industries, 1980).

19. John Corbin, *Developing Computer Based Library Systems* (Phoenix: Oryx Press, 1981), pp. 15–18.

20. A. J. Heindel and H. A. Napier, "Decision Support Systems in Libraries," *Special Libraries* 72 (1981):319–27.

21. J. Akoka, "A Framework For Decision Support Systems Evaluation," *Information and Management* 4 (1981):133–41.

22. M. R. Boomer and R. W. Chorba, *Decision Making for Library Management* (White Plains, NY: Knowledge Industry Publications, Inc., 1982).

23. Charles R. McClure, *Information For Academic Library Decision Making: The Case For Organizational Information Management* (Westport, CT: Greenwood Press, 1980).

24. These two figures are discussed in greater detail in Charles R. McClure, "Management Information for Library Decision Making," in W. Simonton, ed., *Advances in Librarianship,* vol. 12 (New York: Academic Press, 1983).

25. Charles R. McClure, "Planning For Library Services: Lessons and Opportunities," *Journal of Library Administration* 2 (1982):7–28.

26. John V. Richardson, Dennis C. W. Frisch, and Catherine M. Hall, "Bibliographic Organization of U.S. Federal Depository Collections," *Government Publications Review* 7 (1980): 467.

THE EFFECTS OF TECHNOLOGY ON ACCESS TO FEDERAL GOVERNMENT INFORMATION

By Judy E. Myers

Michael Gorman has presented two views of the effect of technology on the future role of the library.[1] He was writing of the transition to online catalogs, but his views seem to apply to the library in general. He called these possible futures the "1984 view" and the "New Jerusalem view."

In the 1984 scenario, technology would mean the end of libraries. Libraries would be doomed to decline, decay, and end in financial ruin. The only role left for them would be as museums for old books. All information will be in electronic form, and everyone will be at home with an Apple VII plugged into the Supersource information network.

In the New Jerusalem scenario, the library would no longer have its cumbersome card catalogs (and perhaps its cumbersome books as well). The librarian would serve as an informed guide, helping users find their way through the trackless realms of electronic information.

Should we expect a major change in library jobs as a result of the transfer of data from print to electronic form? I believe that documents librarians' jobs will be among the first to be affected. Look at what has happened already.

In bibliographic control, the Government Printing Office (GPO) now creates machine-readable records for almost all of the publications received by depository libraries. There is an enormous potential for the use of these records in libraries, and at a cost much less than that of the records for commercially published books.

Changes have also occurred in materials format. Libraries will receive less information from the 1980 Census than from the 1970 Census, in either print or microform. The early plans for the 1980 Census were that libraries would receive less printed information but more in microform. At least, these were the plans as of about 1975. But then the Census Bureau established an entirely new information delivery system, the State Data Center Program, to make the data from the 1980 Census available to the public from computer-readable files.

If one works in a library which serves users with a broad range of interests, this action by the Census Bureau and similar moves by other agencies (for example, the creation of the Department of Energy's RECON database) have made one's job more complicated. The librarian cannot give people as much information from the library's resources as s/he used to. In order to use the new resources, the librarian needs to know whom to call, as well as how to gain access.

This chapter will address the effects of technology on access to bibliographic and government information appearing in new, nonprint forms.

Bibliographic Access

The major manifestations of library technology are the computer-readable bibliographic record and the bibliographic utility. Many libraries have access to the databases of the major bibliographic utilities, OCLC, the Washington Library Network (WLN), and RLIN. Many libraries have, or are planning for, COM or online catalogs. The technology for all of these projects is here today. Whether this technology will help the librarian and users of the library find government publications depends not on the technology but on decisions made both within and outside the library. Chapters 1 and 3 address the decision-making process within the library. In this chapter we will instead discuss the decisions made outside the library—decisions about the quality of cataloging records for documents, whether these records are available when needed, whether they are available on the bibliographic utility in use, what needs to be done so that the library can add records for documents to its (present or future) computer-produced catalog, and what the librarian can do to improve the conditions that affect him or her.

Potential
Even with machine-readable records, the books purchased for the library still have to be cataloged one book at a time. Many libraries used to have

a shortcut for cataloging books in series. They would place standing orders with the Cataloging Distribution Service of the Library of Congress for the card sets of all the publications in a series. For example, a library would ask LC to send card sets for each one of the U.S. Geological Survey Professional Papers. The problem with this system was that all the library received was a set of cards. No machine-readable record was created. And, of course, this process could only be used for materials in series.

How does this relate to documents? The reader may have noticed the connection already. All the publications sent to depository libraries are publications in series, each has an item number that is used to establish a "standing order" with the Government Printing Office. And the catalog records created by the GPO for documents bear the item number as part of the record.

There are companies today which can take the GPO tapes of catalog records, and, using the list of items selected, prepare (a) catalog card sets, (b) a computer-readable tape which can be loaded into the library's online catalog, or (c) a COM catalog of the documents collection.[2] This costs much less than cataloging books one at a time, and it is the only way most libraries will be able even to consider cataloging entire documents collections.

Before librarians are able to take the GPO tapes and load records into the catalog, there are a few things that GPO needs to do to make its records more accurate, to make them compatible with library catalogs, and to make them available wherever they are needed. The easiest way to describe what needs to be done is to give the reader some background on the GPO's cataloging program.

GPO Cataloging

The GPO began to catalog on OCLC in mid-1976. From 1976 through 1980, the GPO operated for the most part like a catalog department—working independently, producing OCLC records that might or might not be consistent with someone else's files. If a name did not appear in LC's name authority file, the GPO established one for its own authority file. LC might later establish the name in a different form. The GPO also did what most catalog departments do—it modified LC subject headings. Sometimes the GPO tagged perfectly good LC subject headings as locally assigned headings, and sometimes it tagged locally invented headings as LC.

Then, in January 1981, the GPO became the center of authority for cataloging federal documents, assuming that role from LC. One effect of the decision was that LC stopped cataloging U.S. documents. Now if LC wants a document cataloged, it sends a request to the GPO. If one is looking for a record of a document cataloged after January 1981, there is no "LC record"; there is instead a "GPO record."

Since January 1981, the GPO has also participated with LC in the Name Authority Cooperative Project. This means that when the GPO assigns a new AACR2 name, the name is added to LC's authority files so that both the GPO and LC will, in the future, use the same one. The GPO also follows LC's cataloging service guidelines in order to produce descriptions consistent with those created by LC.

The LC/GPO collaboration has been beneficial to both agencies, and to all those who use catalog records for documents. Is the SuDocs classification system used in the reader's library? Are there SuDocs numbers on the records from LC? There are a few, but LC usually does not have the SuDocs number. Mentioned earlier was the use of the item number as a means of pulling out groups of records for the documents to be cataloged. Has LC provided item numbers on its catalog records for documents? No, it has not. The GPO, with the support of the Federal Library Committee, the Joint Committee on Printing, and the Catalog Manual Committee of the ALA Government Documents Round Table (GODORT), met with LC and the MARC Format Committee to negotiate changes in some cataloging policies in order to allow the GPO to provide the additional information LC was not providing. Due to these efforts by the GPO, we now have tracings for all the federal agencies responsible for a publication. LC used to limit the number of tracings. This writer remembers one example of a joint publication from the Department of Housing and Urban Development (HUD), the Department of the Interior, and the Department of Health, Education and Welfare. The GPO sent the book to depository libraries with an HH number from HUD. LC provided tracings for two of the three agencies, omitting HUD. LC also does not provide multiple series statements, but the GPO has an agreement with LC by which the GPO can record all of the series statements, no matter how many there are. The GPO also requested and got a MARC field for technical report numbers.

All of that is the good part. Lest it sound as though we have reached bibliographic utopia, let me hasten to note that there are a few problems with the GPO's present cataloging effort. And this is where the librarian comes in. The GPO did not reach this point entirely on its own initiative. Documents librarians asked, even encouraged, the GPO to provide catalog records for documents in such a way that those records would be available to, and acceptable by, libraries. If librarians want to see further progress, they need to tell the GPO what they need, and why these things are important to them.

Subject Cataloging
The GPO is cooperating with LC on descriptive cataloging and on name authorities, but there is one area in which there is not a cooperative

LC/GPO agreement—subject cataloging. When the GPO catalogs a document for LC, it provides LC subject headings for the book, and these are the headings one sees in the *Monthly Catalog* record. When the book gets back to LC, it bypasses the descriptive and name authority process; but it goes to LC's subject catalogers, who may or may not accept the subject headings provided by the GPO. When the librarian later calls up the record for that book on OCLC, he or she may see a different set of subjects.

The GPO-assigned subject headings are valid LC subject headings, assigned in accordance with LC rules. The subject headings on the 1981 and later GPO records should file in any LC subject catalog or load into any computer files without causing problems.

The advantage of an LC/GPO subject collaboration would be higher-quality subject cataloging. GPO catalogers would be able to learn from, and consult with, the LC catalogers in various subjects. The GPO has about two dozen catalogers and one subject specialist. This is a very small group in which to develop a detailed knowledge of the LC subject headings. This is the one area in which the GPO's current cataloging is not as good as LC's. Just compare the subject headings assigned by the GPO with those assigned to the same work by LC. LC usually provides more subject headings, and headings more appropriate to the work.

What would it take to establish a cooperative LC/GPO agreement on subject headings? It would take work on both LC's and the GPO's part, as LC does not have a subject cataloging agreement with any other cataloging agency. Cooperation would both add and save work for LC. LC would have to train the GPO staff and monitor the program to see that the GPO continued to do acceptable subject cataloging. In the long run, LC would almost certainly save time, just as it has saved time by letting the GPO do its name and descriptive cataloging for documents. As with most new programs, time is lost up front, in working out procedures and in training.

We now have LC-quality subject cataloging for the three or four thousand documents which LC adds to its collection each year, and GPO-quality subjects for all the rest of the books cataloged by the GPO. If we as documents users (and taxpayers) want to see good subject cataloging done once, we need to let both LC and the GPO know that this is important to us.

Tape Documentation
Now we come to some problems in GPO procedures that could affect access to records in either a bibliographic utility or a library catalog. Those who use OCLC are very fortunate, because OCLC does not have to load the GPO records from computer tapes. Everyone who has tried

to deal with the tapes has found them to be, well, challenging. This writer has seen anguished letters from Lockheed and WLN describing some of their problems. Let us give a little background for those who do not load tapes every day. Computers do not handle surprises well. They need to be told what to expect. If you tell a computer that certain numbers are MARC field tags and that it is to search for these tags and do certain things with the data in those fields, the computer will recognize only those tags, and only if they are where they belong. Computer tapes in general, not just tapes of catalog records, have information on the tape leader to tell the computer what to expect in the way of data formats, so the computer can select the correct way to proceed.

If there is something new about the tape—for example, if the report numbers were in a 500 field last month, but this month there is a new report number field called 088—the tape should be accompanied by written documentation to tell the people attending the computer what to expect. They can then change the instructions to the computer.

The GPO does not provide tape documentation. There is a certain amount of confusion about where some of the problems arise, because the GPO itself does not sell the tapes. The GPO provides the tapes to LC's Cataloging Distribution Service (CDS). CDS does not use the tapes, so it does not know what documentation is necessary; it just duplicates and sells the tapes. Some of the problems may, or may not, arise from the duplication process; with no documentation, it is hard to tell. But people who have loaded the tapes have reported that some records were unavoidably lost. WLN has only recently (and with a great deal of anguish) loaded the tapes. At least one library that was prepared to use the tapes to put documents records into its online catalog has indefinitely deferred any attempt to use them.

The GPO can correct this problem by providing documentation for its tapes (including the retrospective ones), indicating which MARC tags are used, when new tags were established, and what changes were made in cataloging practices since the last tape. The GPO tapes need the same kinds of documentation as the cataloging tapes produced by LC. This will be a moderately big job, but it can be approached in stages. The first step should be to start providing documentation for the current tapes. Priority should then be given to documenting the tapes retrospectively to January 1981 and then back to 1976.

Error Correction
Whether or not errors in the library's catalog are corrected is determined by the library. It is a decision that affects the library and its users. Most libraries correct some errors in their catalogs and ignore others. For example, would most libraries retype a record to remove an extra space

between two characters? If the library has an online catalog, and the computer will not search a call number if the spacing is wrong, the policy would almost certainly be to correct the error. But, if the library has a card catalog, an extra space does not matter—at least, not right away.

This writer studied a small sample of the documents cataloging records in the OCLC database prepared by LC and by the GPO during 1980, the last year before the changes to AACR2. Both the GPO and LC were making about two errors per cataloging record. The error rate must surely have increased during the transition to AACR2, but the number of errors is not really the point here. The point is that both LC and the GPO make errors. LC distributes a tape of error corrections; the GPO does not. The GPO corrects its book catalog, but not its machine-readable records in OCLC and its own tapes. Suppose the GPO finds an error after the *Monthly Catalog* has been printed. The GPO has decided that only certain types of errors will be corrected in the retrospective *Monthly Catalogs*, including errors in SuDoc and item numbers. The GPO would print these corrections in a later edition of the *Monthly Catalog*. The GPO has sometimes corrected SuDoc numbers in the OCLC database, but there is no documentation to tell us what kinds of errors were corrected during which time periods. We do know that the GPO does not correct any errors on the tapes after the tapes leave the GPO. The GPO has not even implemented a mechanism to make these corrections.

The lack of error correction is serious for two reasons. First, if the GPO does not correct the typos and other cataloging errors, librarians themselves will have to try to find and correct the errors in order to have correct records for their own catalogs. Second, if the item numbers are missing from the records because publications were cataloged before an item number was assigned, librarians will not be able to use an item number search to retrieve groups of records for materials to be cataloged.

It would not be difficult for the GPO to produce a tape of corrections. The GPO could use the same procedure any OCLC library uses to correct its archive tapes. Let us look at the tape process from the beginning. A GPO cataloger keys an original cataloging record into the OCLC database, then presses the "produce" key on the terminal. Pressing the "produce" key causes that original cataloging record to be copied into the OCLC database and onto GPO's archive tape. OCLC sends these archive tapes to the GPO, which in turn uses the tapes to produce the *Monthly Catalog*. Suppose the GPO finds an error while the *Monthly Catalog* is being edited. It corrects the error so that the printed *Monthly Catalog* will be correct. Now, here is the procedure for correcting the OCLC database and the tape: all the GPO needs to do is to make the correction in the OCLC database, then press the "update" key. This will create a corrected record on a separate tape, which can then be distributed to tape subscribers—with appropriate written documentation!

As our national cataloging authority for documents, the GPO has a responsibility to correct its cataloging errors. This will obviously cost money, but how much more will it cost for each librarian to try to find and correct these errors?

Microform Cataloging

Have you noticed that the *Monthly Catalog* frequently provides a description for a printed copy, when the library received a microform? This happens when the GPO received a printed copy and filmed it for distribution. The description a librarian sees gives the number of pages and the size in centimeters of the printed copy. It does not give the number of microfiches, whether the fiches are negative or positive, or their reduction ratio. The catalog record does not match the publication the library receives. The printed copy is going to the National Archives, and the GPO has created a catalog record for that one library. The rest of the 1,365 depository libraries that might have received that document are going to have to redo the descriptive part of the record. The GPO catalogs the printed copy because that is the form in which it receives the document.[3] But to catalog printed copies when depository libraries receive microforms is the wrong decision. It means that each librarian who wants to use that record will have to change it. This is contrary to the whole principle of national-level cataloging. The GPO should provide microform records for materials distributed in microform, printed copy records for documents distributed in print, and two records for the publications distributed to some libraries in print and to others in microform.

The Librarian's Role

A moderately long list has been given of bibliographic control problems: subject cataloging, tape documentation, error correction, and microform cataloging. We said earlier that the librarian can play a role in improving these situations. He or she can let the GPO know how these matters affect library operations. The Superintendent of Documents, Raymond Mason Taylor, has spoken very strongly of his intention to improve the depository library system.[4] He is not a cataloger, and these topics must seem as obscure to him as they do at first to most librarians. If a library uses the WLN or the RLIN cataloging utility, or if it might want to buy and use the GPO tapes, someone should tell Mr. Taylor how important it is that it have tape documentation. If the library plans to use the GPO records at all—on a bibliographic utility, on DIALOG, or in-house—tell Mr. Taylor how important it is to have corrections made to the OCLC records and the tapes, how important it is for the GPO to go back and add or correct item numbers, and to describe microforms as microforms.

Benefits
The whole idea of national-level cataloging is so that, if the GPO creates a correct record, each librarian does not have to redo it. The GPO spends a lot of time and money to do almost everything right. It is giving the library community high-quality records, with name and subject authorities consistent with LC practice (and thus, consistent with the files in most libraries). The GPO planned to eliminate its cataloging backlog by the end of the 1982 calendar year. If GPO records were as accurate as those of LC, most libraries could select groups of records from the GPO tapes by item number, and could accept them with only clerical review. At the University of Houston Library (UH), this procedure would cost about $1.40 per cataloged document. But, if the records must be processed one at a time through the OCLC terminal (because the item numbers are not on the tapes or are not correct), and if each record has to be checked by a skilled technician (with a certain proportion being routed to a cataloger), the cost at UH would be closer to $4.50 per document. In today's economy, in most libraries, that figure could easily make the difference between being able to consider cataloging documents or not. At UH there are about 110,000 titles with GPO cataloging records. At $1.40 each, records could be added to the online catalog for $154,000. If the GPO does not correct its errors, the cost to UH would be $495,000.

New Formats and Distribution Methods

Mentioned earlier were the Census Bureau's State Data Center Program and the Department of Energy's RECON database. A report published five years ago by the National Commission on Library and Information Science estimated that at that time there were approximately 10,000 to 12,000 federal statutes requiring that information be collected.[5] What happened to this information? The federal government is the world's largest user of computers and computer equipment, and much of that computer power is used to tabulate and analyze the results of these information-gathering efforts. The traditional formats for distributing this information have been paper and microfiche.

But the Census Bureau's State Data Center Program indicates that we have entered a new era. In 1970 it was undoubtedly less expensive to publish the results of the Census in considerable detail, rather than to provide computer searches to retrieve the subset of data a person might need. By 1980 the balance had shifted. In the late 1970s and early 1980s,

Census Bureau representatives at library meetings reported that micro-publishing the data from some of the census tapes would result in collections of 50,000 microfiches for one tape, 25,000 microfiches for another, etc. Martha Wyeth of the Census Bureau, in September 1982, reported sample costs of $41 million for depository distribution, in microfiche, of the data from STF 1A plus the ED maps. STF 3A would cost $46 million, etc.[6] And those figures do not include the cost of a library's microfiche cabinets, floor space, or microfiche readers. The decision, announced in September 1982, was that these micropublications would not be distributed to depository libraries.[7] There will apparently be more negotiation, however, so watch the GPO *Administrative Notes* for new information.

The Census Bureau example illustrates a process that is going on throughout the federal government. Even when the data are going to be heavily used, it is becoming more expensive—at least in the short run—to distribute a product than to provide a direct information service. Where the information is less heavily used, the decision is even easier to make. The Center on Aging established a small depository system for research reports on aging. At first the Center announced that a printed index to the collection would be provided. Then it decided to maintain the index in one place—Washington—and to have users call for a search of the card file.

There are several important economic points to be made about this process. The first is that libraries and users in many cases have to pay for the computer search or the telephone call to Washington. Second, data centers and people to search card files have to be funded continuously. It may not, in the long run, be cheaper to fund a service rather than a product, but there is tremendous pressure on agencies to reduce their present budgets. It is very difficult for agencies to justify their public information services, or their publications, at all.

That brings us to the political aspects of this topic, of which there are two: (1) the present law affecting depository libraries and (2) the information policy of the present administration.

Laws and Government Policy
For the past several years depository libraries have been able to select an excellent series of foreign language textbooks, prepared for the Foreign Service Institute of the State Department. There are accompanying audio tapes, which are essential for use of the books. Depository libraries receive the books but not the tapes. The tapes are classified as audiovisual materials, and audiovisual materials have not been included in the depository program. The library community sought to have Title 44 of the *United States Code* revised a few years ago. One of the most controversial proposals in the revision was the inclusion of audiovisual and

machine-readable information in the depository library system. The proposed revision failed.

Another law that affects depository libraries was recently enacted — the Paperwork Reduction Act of 1980. This innocuously titled law gives the Office of Management and Budget (OMB) a great deal of authority to regulate the public availability of government information. One of OMB's first actions under the law was to declare a moratorium on all new government periodicals, pamphlets, and audiovisual materials. An OMB representative reported at the ALA Annual Conference in June 1982 that the moratorium had a greater impact than even OMB expected, and that some of the information OMB felt should have been distributed to the public had been stopped. When asked whether OMB had clarified its request to the agencies, the response was no, that OMB had too many other things to do.[8] The clearest statement I have seen of the potential effect of the Paperwork Reduction Act and OMB's activities was in a presentation by Mr. Kenneth Allen of the OMB, in the April 1981 transcript of the meeting of the Depository Library Council to the Public Printer.[9]

OMB affects the dissemination of government information in any form. Title 44, and the regulations which interpret it, control whether the depository libraries have access to anything other than paper or microfiche.

GPO Role

The Depository Library Council, at its Spring 1982 meeting in Boston, requested that the GPO ask the Joint Committee on Printing (JCP) to "...review Title 44 for changes necessary to update the definition of 'government information' to encompass new technologies...."[10] The response of GPO's General Council in September 1982 was: "There would seem to be little authority or precedent for [this] request."[11] What this means is that if depository librarians want to access information in new forms, they, as constituents of the user community, need to approach Congress and, specifically, the Joint Committee on Printing, not the GPO.

JCP Role

The Congressional Joint Committee on Printing has expressed an interest in making some minor revisions to Title 44, since its proposed major revision failed. Faye Padgett, the Assistant Staff Director of the Joint Committee on Printing, reported at the September 1982 meeting of the Depository Library Council that, as part of its plan to revise Title 44, the JCP will establish a study committee on access by depository libraries to federal databases. The goal of the committee is to make recommendations ensuring public access to federal information.[12]

The Librarian's Role
This is an important issue, with plenty of knotty aspects. If one focuses on the economic and other obstacles confronting the 1,365 depository libraries trying to dial up a database on a federal computer, it is tempting to say that the whole idea is too far out, that it will not work. This writer tries to approach this topic by thinking of herself as the link between the user and the information. The librarian may not have the computer, or the tape, or even the terminal in his or her library. But all librarians have a telephone, and with that and a planned system of access, they can have the information.

What can the librarian do about this issue? He or she can tell the chair of the JCP what is being done to provide federal information to the public, and what information resources are needed for the job to continue to be done. If the librarian resides in a state where the Census Bureau does not have a data center, or where the data center is not effective or charges too much for users; if the library's users need access to a federal database in order to get information necessary for their work or their research, let the chair of the JCP know.

New information technology does not always cost more than the present means of access; sometimes it *saves* money. The U.S. Department of the Interior is investigating the feasibility of distributing the U.S. Geological Survey topographic maps on videodiscs. The 54,000 U.S. topographic maps would fit on one videodisc.[13] Videodisc players cost money, but so do map cases. The library would not be able to receive these discs under the present interpretation of Title 44. Will the discs meet the needs of users? For example, can distances be measured accurately? Can the maps be copied? Or will videodisc maps be useful only as a browsing file, to be followed by a need for a printed copy? If the library uses topographic maps, let the Joint Committee on Printing know what concerns and questions it has.

Conclusion

At the beginning of this chapter, Michael Gorman's two views of the future were mentioned. Here are a few more.

Christopher Evans recently wrote a popular book entitled *The Micro Millenium*.[14] Evans envisioned not only the demise of the book, but of the professions as well. He observed that the special strength of a professional, such as a librarian, is exclusive knowledge in a specific area. The raw material of a modern profession is information, and the expertise of a professional lies in knowing the rules. In Evans' future, the computerized equivalent of an article or book can be transmitted electronically to the terminal in one's home, where the information can be permanently stored in a computer chip. The "rules" for finding information will be handled by a computerized reference inquiry, modeled on those already in use for medical diagnosis, mineral exploration, chemical analysis, and many other purposes.[15,17]

Anthony Smith presents the opposite view of the future in *Goodbye Gutenberg*.[18] Smith and Evans agree on many points, such as consumer demand to own rather than share resources, the ready availability of electronic information in the home, and the prospective increase in the market for electronic gadgets. But Smith sees the library as increasing in power, because the librarian "chooses the codes in which to categorize information, and arranges the key words through which the information can be extracted. The librarian becomes in a sense the sentinel at the gateway of information and knowledge. Who has made the computer-librarian lord and master over knowledge, and how is his stewardship supervised and rendered accountable to society?"[19] This writer would like to ask Mr. Smith's rhetorical question of OMB.

I believe libraries can find themselves in either of these futures, and our present actions can help to determine our future. The federal government is becoming very aware that information is money and information is power. The policy of our present government is to control the dissemination of information. Kenneth Allen stated that OMB's primary goal was to reduce the cost of government by cutting unnecessary activities. When asked where informing the public ranked in OMB's priorities, he replied that public information was an important goal, "but sometimes goals conflict and we cannot afford everything we would like to do."[20] That is obviously a true statement, but it can easily be used as the argument for restricting public information for the purposes of power and control.

Libraries are remarkably resilient institutions. The printed book was supposed to mean the end of libraries—with books so numerous, everyone who could read could have their own. The printed book turned out to be the end of scribes, not of libraries. Then came radio, which was supposed to be the end of reading. People still read, although television has perhaps made a greater impact than radio. So it is tempting to be complacent, to say that we will be here after the electronic information fad has passed.

I believe this trend is different. Libraries are funded, not to provide services to people who cannot afford books, but to serve those who cannot otherwise access the information they need, when they need it. Libraries exist because publishers do not keep books and magazines in stock for immediate delivery upon request. Libraries serve the information-rich to a much greater extent than they serve the information-poor. Libraries cannot successfully justify their existence by arguing that they provide services to people who cannot afford books or home computers with which to access databases. The people who support libraries are the people who have access to other resources, but who need libraries, too. If these people have direct access to books and magazines through their own terminals, then their major need for libraries will become their need for an informed guide through Michael Gorman's and Anthony Smith's trackless realms of database access codes, thesauruses, and search protocols.

Documents librarians have an additional responsibility—to raise public awareness of the value of federal information. They have been doing that for years, and successfully, too. The depository program has come a long way. Librarians are receiving more and more of the printed information provided by the government. Now they must broaden their view, and play the same role in improving public access, by new means, to new forms of information.

References

1. Michael Gorman, "The Prospective Catalog," in *Closing the Catalog: Proceedings of the 1978 and 1979 Library and Information Technology Associates Institutes* (Phoenix, AR: Oryx Press, 1980), p. 85.

2. Two such companies are Marcive (San Antonio, Texas), (512) 828-9496—contact person, Jim Plaunt, and Informatics (Rockville, Maryland), (301) 770-3000—contact person, Penny Glassman.

3. Personal communication with Stuart Greenberg.

4. Raymond Mason Taylor, in *Depository Library Council to the Public Printer, Transcript of the Fall 1982 Meeting*, pp. 10–29. The transcript is to be distributed in microfiche to all depository libraries. The SuDoc classification number is GP 3.30:982/2.

5. U.S. Domestic Council, Committee on the Right of Privacy, *National Information Policy: Report to the President of the United States* (Washington, DC: National Commission on Libraries and Information Science, 1977), p. 25. The SuDoc number is Y3.L61:2In3/2.

6. Martha Wyeth, in *Depository Library Council. . .Fall 1982 Meeting*, pp. 219–20.

7. Ibid., pp. 220–21.

8. Robert N. Deedor, American Library Association Annual Conference, Government Documents Round Table, Federal Documents Task Force Program, July 12, 1982.

9. Kenneth Allen, in *Depository Library Council. . .Transcript of the Spring 1981 Meeting*, pp. 303–55. Distributed to all depository libraries in microfiche, SuDoc number GP 3.30:981.

10. Resolution 24, *Depository Library Council...Transcript of the Spring 1982 Meeting*, appendix. To be distributed to all depository libraries in microfiche, SuDoc number GP 3.30:982.

11. General Counsel, Government Printing Office, "Opinion concerning the appropriateness of referring certain resolutions of the Depository Library Council to the Joint Committee on Printing," September 17, 1982, in *Depository Library Council...Fall 1982 Meeting*, appendix.

12. Faye Padgett, in *Depository Library Council...Fall 1982 Meeting*, pp. 33–35.

13. Gary North in *Depository Library Council...Fall 1982 Meeting*, pp. 165–68.

14. Christopher Evans, *The Micro Millenium* (New York, Washington Square Press, paperback, 1981). *See* chapter 8 ("The Death of the Printed Word") and chapter 9 ("The Decline of the Professions").

15. Richard O. Dula and John G. Gaschnig, "Knowledge-Based Expert Systems Come of Age," *Byte* 6 (September 1981): 238–81. This survey article has an extensive bibliography.

16. Pamela McCorduck, *Machines Who Think: A Personal Inquiry into the History and Prospects of Artificial Intelligence* (San Francisco: W. H. Freeman and Company, 1979). *See* chapter 12, "Applied Artificial Intelligence."

17. Donald Michie, *Expert Systems in the Micro-electronic Age* (Edinburgh: Edinburgh University Press, 1979). He provides detailed descriptions of several systems.

18. Anthony Smith, *Goodbye Gutenberg: The Newspaper Revolution of the 1980's* (New York: Oxford University Press, 1980). *See* chapter 8, "An Electronic Alexandria."

19. Ibid., p. 314.

20. Allen, in *Depository Library Council...*, p. 328.

ATTITUDES, RESOURCES, AND APPLICATIONS: THE GOVERNMENT DOCUMENTS LIBRARIAN AND COMPUTER TECHNOLOGY

By Bruce Morton

Before discussing the automated systems I have developed at Carleton College, I would like to offer my views on why documents librarianship has been so slow to embrace automation. For the last two years I have served as coordinator of the American Library Association's Government Documents Round Table's Machine-Readable Government Information Task Force. It has become abundantly clear to me that documents librarians, by and large, have shown little interest in the Task Force or the concerns it addresses.

Attitudes

Recently, while paging through the various papers of the *Proceedings of the Second National Conference of the Association of College and Research Libraries,*[1] I came across the paper "Options for the 80s [the theme of the conference]: How Does the Documents Librarian Meet the Challenges of the 1980s?"[2] In it, Ruth Dahlgren Hartman, documents librarian at

Central Washington University, refers to the computer as the "miracle" of the 1980s for documents librarianship.[3] Let us hope she is correct. For if she is, this computer "miracle" will be for documents librarians similar to the one their colleagues in most other areas of librarianship experienced during the previous decade.

Librarians have too long refrained from entering the technological mainstream of their profession. In this case, they cannot conveniently use the U.S. Government Printing Office (GPO) as their scapegoat. I know it is fashionable for speakers and writers on documents topics to focus attention on the GPO as the source of all woes. I am writing here, however, neither to praise nor to criticize the GPO. For, in my opinion, the cause of our situation *vis-à-vis* computer technology is no more the fault of the GPO than it is of any single documents librarian. Documents librarianship is the sum of all the profession's successes and failures; therefore, all must bear collective blame for the predicament of being mired in a technological backwater, while the rest of librarianship is swept up by the technological current. The various individual efforts which have been made to automate certain aspects of documents operations have all failed to be synthesized into readily adoptable, adaptable, and transportable systems.[4] I find it puzzling, for instance, that no one has shown the initiative and entrepreneurship to produce and distribute a microcomputer program on a floppy disk (say, for an Apple II) for the automation of items files. In short, to characterize the situation, I paraphrase the immortal Pogo, "We meet the enemy and they, unfortunately, are us."

The initial step documents librarians must take is one of confrontation. But before confronting library administrations, they must confront themselves. Whether their past neglect, intentional avoidance, and personal reticence have been caused by ignorance, anxiety (cyberphobia, for those who speak computerese), lack of imagination, fiscal reality, or any combination of these factors, the cause must first be recognized and then addressed. It is my hope that I may, in some way, prod, stimulate or raise individual and collective consciousness – and collective conscience – toward this end. I do not expect to create computer zealots (cyberphrenes, in the jargon), but rather to encourage a willingness and a desire to consider what the computer, whether it be a mainframe or micro, can do for us. There is nothing intrinsically good about the computer or its use. While one must guard against being made to feel a "Luddite" if one chooses not to use the computer, one must realize that the computer is nothing more than a *tool*. As such, it must be considered in light of how it might be used – what might be built and accomplished with it.

Resources

There is much we might, and should, accomplish with the computer that we do not and cannot do by manual means. Of course, each library must decide what needs to be done and what its priorities are. Software, hardware, and cost will be quite different depending on whether priorities lie with online public access or with librarian-oriented management systems. In either case, the computer provides a way to accomplish what might not even have been thought of previously because the means were not then available.

The computer presents the depository librarian with a valuable and heretofore relatively untapped tool. Even the rudimentary first step of a records management system that automates active (see Figure 3-1) and inactive item files has had a noticeably positive impact on my own efforts to develop and manage the collection. This is nothing more than simple list processing. It is an ideal place for anyone, or any library considering computer applications for its depository operations, to begin. As a matter of fact, I cannot understand why every depository does not strive to automate its items files at the earliest possible moment. The benefits of automation are obvious and irrefutable. And, of course, a residual benefit is that it provides an excellent introductory appreciation of the power of even the simplest of computer applications.

Until the implementation of the automated item files system, documents librarians had to think of the development of the depository collection in a linear context—lines of cards in various disjoint active and inactive files that represented growing rows of documents on the shelf.

Conceptually, collection development had become the process of building and keeping various card files. There was little sense of relationships amongst the separate card files. The limitations of card stock, oak drawer, and pull rod keep files and the process of collection development physically and conceptually separate as well. Automation, however, permits—even invites—the librarian to perceive the dynamics of addition, rejection, deletion, and discontinuance as aspects of a continuing and fluid process of collection development and management, each part of which is inextricably related to the other parts.[5] For instance, when several item classes are deleted by the depository library or discontinued by GPO, consideration must be given to what weakness, if any, the future absence of the kind of material generated by those item classes will cause the collection. The computer provides an instrument by which the processes of collection development may be better monitored, understood and, consequently, managed.

The capability to extract from item files profiles of document holdings based on authoring agency, truncated SuDoc classification, date of

Figure 3-1: Sample Record Output from Automated Active Items File (IACT)*

```
ITEM:       900-C-14
SUDOC:      S18.53:
TITLE:      COUNTRY PROFILES (SERIES) [FICHE] AGENCY FOR INT'L DEV
SURVEY:     81-74
DATADD:     28JAN82
CARLETON HOLDS:   YES        ST. OLAF HOLDS:     NO
CARLETON RATING:  1          ST. OLAF RATING:    2
```

*Carleton College and St. Olaf College holdings notation allows the file to serve as a union list of active item classes. Carleton and St. Olaf ratings notation relate to the joint collection development activities of the two depositories. Rating categories are: 1=essential; 2=desired held by one or other depository, but not by both; 3=don't care. For fuller discussion see endnotes 5 and 6.

initial active status, survey number, and holding symbol and ratings codes for another depository,[6] gives documents librarians the capability to better inform themselves, as well as their colleagues involved in collection development for serials and monographs, about the ways in which the U.S. government publications interface with the library's total collection. If so desired, the automation of documents records in a shelflist, public catalog, or items file can serve as the foundation for cooperative collection development between depository libraries. (This seems particularly appropriate since 50 percent of depository libraries are located within ten miles of each other.) But, to automate item files as an exercise in and of itself is not adequate. The information gathered from such an analysis must be related to titles on the shelf.

Applications

Turning from the concept of item class to the actual titles on the shelf that come as the result of item class subscription, it should be mentioned that at Carleton College we have a working prototype for an automated shelflist (see Figure 3-2). The automated shelflist enables us to determine, for example, which item classes over a period of time are producing pamphlet material and in what amounts they are producing such material. This information is found by searching FLAG fields for a cue for pamphlet material and then sorting and summing the output by item class. Or, merely the summing of item classes within a particular time period will provide an item class productivity profile which indicates how many physical titles are resulting from each item class selected.[7]

The major bibliographic utilities, such as OCLC and RLIN, as well as GPO's *Monthly Catalog* tapes, provide access to MARC format, bibliographic documents records. For most depository libraries, however, the prospect of fully utilizing the potential services of these utilities is not economically feasible. Full cataloging of the relatively large number of documents titles received annually by even a small depository is prohibitively expensive, regardless of whether cataloging is done by automated or manual means (except on a very selective basis). Also to be considered, in the case of OCLC or RLIN, are first-time use fees as well as the labor intensity of the cooperative obligation to delete holdings symbols upon the withdrawal of a title from the collection. This latter issue is a particularly important concern for small selective depositories, where collections tend to be fluid.

It is apparent at this time that most depositories do not rely on catalogs, automated or manual, as the primary means of gaining access to their documents collection. In fact, two-thirds of all depository libraries

Figure 3-2: Data Entry Workform for Automated Shelflist (SL) Record*

```
DTR> STORE SL
Enter SUDOC:
Enter MF-HC:
Enter TITLE:
Enter AUTHOR:
Enter DATPUB:
Enter DATRCV:
Enter SHPLST:
Enter ITEM:
Enter DEPOS:
Enter HOLDNG:
Enter LCCALL:
Enter FLAG1:
Enter FLAG2:
Enter NOTE:
```

*Fields in descending order are: (1) Superintendent of Documents (SuDoc) classification; (2) Microfiche or paper copy; (3) Title; (4) Date of publication; (5) Date received; (6) Shipping list number; (7) Item class number; (8) Received under depository program, yes or no; (9) Holding library, Carleton College and/or St. Olaf College; (10) Library of Congress Classification, if cataloged; (11 & 12) Flag fields allow coded input, e.g., PAM = pamphlet, REF = reference, SER = serial, DAT = dated or superseded, CRR = current reading room. For lengthier discussion of the shelflist system and record content see endnote 7.

find it necessary to purchase commercial documents indexes in order to fully utilize depository materials.[8] It is not unusual for depository receipts to exceed book receipts annually by as much as 200 percent even in a small depository; this output effectively militates against affordable input and local online storage. Yet for those unique libraries which decide to undertake massive integration of documents into an online catalog, documents librarians should ensure that adequate consideration is given to record enhancements indicating date received, format cues (e.g., pamphlet, map, serial), and depository or nondepository status of the document. Local fields within a system (e.g., OCLC's 590, 910, and 949 fields) could be used for such purposes. If this is done, catalog records could still be manipulated by management software packages in order to target and profile material based on format, supersession, date received, or other relevant factors specific to U.S. government documents librarianship.

In any case, libraries must determine whether to buy an automated system in order to avoid a headache, or whether they are buying a headache which will in the end manage them (see Figures 3-3, 3-3A, and 3-4).

Under current conditions, medium to small depository libraries cannot and will not avail themselves of the opportunities for automation of depository operations through existing cooperative utilities. Many libraries cling to depository status only because they are able to rationalize a cost/benefit ratio in their favor. The costs inherent in buying machine-readable records from a utility, considering the volume of depository material annually processed, would seriously endanger the precarious balance between cost and benefit for many of these libraries. Yet, at the same time, libraries can ill afford, either for reasons of economy or public service, to permit their documents collections to grow by a process of uncontrolled accretion. Relatively uncomplicated in-house management systems can fulfill important needs for the small to medium depository until the GPO, the major utilities, or private sector vendors address the particular needs and resources of selective depository libraries.

Space is a preeminent concern for all areas of the library, but for none more so than a documents collection. This is because documents librarians deal directly with the world's most prolific publisher, the U.S. Government Printing Office, the products of which mirror the vagaries of bureaucratic expansion and contraction, policy formulation and change, and, as we are all now acutely aware, budget considerations. Among documents librarians there is a constant awareness of the possibility of being imminently deluged by government documentation. Documents librarians, therefore, must be concerned continually with how best to ensure the acquisition of materials appropriate to a library's predetermined needs and how judiciously to develop that collection in order to maintain maximum utility. The collection must be regularly scrutinized for titles no longer relevant to the desired collection profile or to the present and projected needs of users. Too often, only the acquisition of material and its appearance on the shelf have been assumed as evidence of active collection development, while shelving, reshelving, weeding, and processing material have been assumed to represent collection management. This, of course, is not true. Collection development is much more than the mere selection of item classes and the shelving of the titles those item classes generate. Rather, collection development is the process of management decision making that will determine the specific materials or categories of materials to be obtained and retained.[9]

At Carleton College we wish to maximize management decision making. Pamphlets, for instance, are a format which our collection development policy explicitly states will not be collected.[10] Our collection

Figure 3-3: OCLC Record for Document NF3.2:L61*

NO HOLDINGS IN MNN – FOR HOLDINGS ENTER dh DEPRESS DISPLAY RECD SEND
OCLC: 7139253   Rec stat: n Entrd: 810219   Used: 820419
Type: a Bib lvl: m Govt pub: f Lang: eng Source: d Illus: k
Repr: Enc lvl: I Conf pub: 0 Ctry: dcu Dat tp: s M/F/B: 00
Indx: 0 Mod rec: Festschr: 0 Cont:
Desc: a Int lvl: Dates: 1980,

```
 1  010
 2  040       GPO c GPO
 3  043       n-us---
 4  074       831-B-1
 5  086    0  NF 3.2:L 61
 6  090       b
 7  049       MNNA
 8  245   00  Humanities projects in libraries / c National Endowment for the Humanities, Division of Public Programs.
 9  260    0  Washington, D.C. : b The Endowment, c [1980?]
10  300       1 folded sheet (5 p.) : b forms ; c 23 cm.
11  500       Cover title.
12  650    0  Federal aid to libraries.
13  650    0  Libraries x Cultural programs.
14  650    0  Endowments z United States.
15  710   20  National Endowment for the Humanities. b Division of Public Programs.
```

*Field 300 indicates pamphlet character of the document but offers no flagging device to recall on that basis. There is also no indication in the record that the last application deadline is 15 July 1981; therefore, even though this document may be withdrawn from the collection after that date under depository guidelines, there is no way to recall the record on that basis either. Likewise, there is no specified field to indicate the date when the document was received; consequently it cannot be recalled after the expiration of the statutory five-year retention period.

Figure 3-3A: The Cover and Page [3] of Document NF3.2:L61*

National Endowment for the Humanities
Division of Public Programs

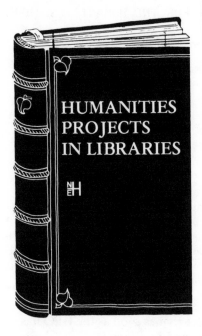

HUMANITIES
PROJECTS
IN LIBRARIES

N
E
H

14,462   6-23-80

Eligibility

To be eligible for funding, a project should:
- focus on the humanities or provide the perspective of the humanities on an issue or topic;
- include public participation in project activities;
- aim primarily at an adult out-of-school audience;
- involve the use of specific humanities resources belonging to a library—its books, media, services, and staff, with a view to continued and increased use of these library resources once the project is completed;
- include knowledgeable and appropriate resource people in the planning and implementation of the program such as: librarians, subject specialists, technical experts, and community representatives.

Deadlines—Applications Receipt

July 15, 1980
October 15, 1980
January 15, 1981
July 15, 1981

NATIONAL ENDOWMENT
  FOR THE HUMANITIES
DIVISION OF PUBLIC PROGRAMS
HUMANITIES PROJECTS IN LIBRARIES
MAIL STOP 406 - 806 15TH STREET, NW
WASHINGTON, D.C.
Telephone (202) 724-0760

*Page [3] indicates a series of application deadlines after which the document ceases to have general utility.

Figure 3-4: Automated Shelflist (SL) Record for Document NF3.2:L61*

```
DTR> FIND SL WITH SUDOC="NF3.2:L61"
[1 Record found]
DTR> LIST
SUDOC:   NF3.2:L61
MF-HC:   HC
TITLE:   HUMANITIES PROJECTS IN LIBRARIES
AUTHOR:  NATIONAL ENDOWMENT FOR THE HUMANITIES (NEH)
DATPUB:  31DEC80
DATRCV:  30JUN80
SHPLST:  14462
ITEM:    831 B1
DEPOS:   Y
HOLDNG:  CS
LCCALL:
FLAG1:   PAM
FLAG2:   DAT
NOTE:    APPLICATION DEADLINE 15JUL81, THEN W/D.
```

*FLAG1 indicates that document is a pamphlet, and FLAG2 that it is dated. The note field states that the application deadline for the program advertised by document is 15 JUL81, and that after that date it should be withdrawn. This information is input with initial data input and can be used to recall the document by searching flag field(s) alone or in combination with any other field(s).

development policy also explicitly states that as soon as the GPO has discontinued an item class or we have deleted an active item, all titles in the collection that have been received as a result of subscription to that item class will be immediately reviewed for withdrawal. Again, a search of the shelflist via item field will produce the targeted titles (see Figures 3-5 and 3-6). The list can further be honed by factoring in a command that will eliminate all titles received in the last five years, thereby assuring compliance with the statutory retention obligation. Those titles that have been in the collection for less than five years may be flagged for later review with the cuing FLAG "RVW." Titles reviewed for whatever reason, of course, can be further limited by intersecting with specifications of other fields by means of Boolean operators. It is also quite possible to institute a daily review of all material received five years ago. Titles can, therefore, be immediately considered for withdrawal on the day they become eligible (see Figure 3-7).

Figure 3-5: Search of Shelflist (SL) for Pamphlet Material*

```
DRT> FIND SL WITH FLAG1="PAM" OR FLAG2="PAM"
[58 Records found]
DTR> SORT BY ITEM
DTR> SUM 1 BY ITEM
```

ITEM	
- -	8
1051-B-20	1
1062-C	5
1089- -	1
128 - -	1
150 - -	1
429 -B-	2
431 -I-1	7
461 -A-1	1
467 -A-3	1
474 -A-1	1
486 -E-1	1
497 -C-2	1
535 - -	1
580 -B-	1
582 - -	6
583 - -	1
603 - -	1
609 -C-1	1
612 - -	5
646 -C-	1

*Pamphlet records are then sorted and output on the basis of item class. The resultant profile allows the documents librarian to see which item classes produce the most pamphlet material. Those item classes may then be scrutinized for continuation or deletion from the active items file (IACT, *see* Figure 3-1).

Figure 3-6: Surveying Pamphlet Productivity Profile*

```
DTR> FIND SL WITH ITEM="612"
[8 Records found]
DTR> PRINT ALL SUDOC


                        SUDOC

        I49.2:AS7
        I49.2:D85/4
        I49.2:EC7/8/V.2
        I49.2:EC7/8/V.3
        I49.2:EC7/8/V.4
        I49.2:EN2/10
        I49.2:L22
        I49.2:W29/18
```

Shelflist (SL) is searched on basis of item class (in this case, item class 612) in order to ascertain which pamphlet titles were received because of subscription to item class 612. SuDoc class is printed for all titles, whereupon they may be retrieved from stacks and considered for retention or withdrawal.

Microfiche, especially, can be a beneficiary of automation. The promise offered by an automated records management system bodes well for documents librarians who have to confront the problems of collection management resulting from GPO's now considerable micro-publishing program. Microfiche, by its very nature, demands special treatment in order to preserve, access, and manage it. No longer will documents librarians be able to get by with infrequent shelf reading to ascertain which material should be considered for retention or with-drawal. Microfiches, even more than hardcopy documents, tend to accrete. Since microform material does not usually circulate, librarians cannot rely on circulation records as an indication of the relative useful-ness of specific microformatted documents. Also there are no dogeared pages to reveal use. Conversely, there is no dust accumulation to suggest lack of use. However, automated records management systems will at least allow documents librarians to review a microfiche collection by invoking the field that indicates microform or paper format. At that point the part of the microfiche collection to be targeted can be limited by the Boolean intersection of any of several fields in order to elicit microfiche holdings that have the desired profile[11] (see Figure 3-8).

**Figure 3-7: Automated Shelflist (SL) Record
Returned on a Search for Documents Received Five Years Ago
(10 August 1982, i.e., on 10 August 1977)***

```
DTR> FIND SL WITH DATRCV="10AUG77"
[1 Record found]
DTR> LIST

SUDOC:  EP1.2:W29/42
MF-HC:  HC
TITLE:  CLEAN WATER & CANE SUGAR INDUSTRY
AUTHOR: EPA
DATPUB: 31-APR-77
DATRCV: 10-AUG-77
SHPLST: 10014
ITEM:   431 -I-1
DEPOS:  Y
HOLDNG: C
LCCALL:
FLAG1:  RVW
FLAG2:  PAM
NOTE:
```

*The automated shelflist was designed so there could be a daily review of material received five years ago and so that the material could be reviewed for possible retention or withdrawal from the collection on the day a document becomes eligible for withdrawal.

Implementation

Libraries can assess the viability of automation of documents operations by:

- Developing and producing a statement of collection management goals and objectives
- Developing, producing, and implementing a well thought-out collection development and management policy
- Consulting with librarians experienced in library computer applications, and, if at all possible, with documents librarians who are so experienced

**Figure 3-8: An Added Feature of the Automated
Shelflist (SL) Is Label Generation***

```
DTR> FIND SL WITH SHPLST="12644"
[1 Record found]
DTR> :LABEL
```

```
Y3.T22/2:2N88/2
EFFECTS OF NUCLEAR WAR

              CARLETON COLLEGE
                 LIBRARY
              U.S. DEPOSITORY

1070-M-          12644              21-JUN-79
```

*The self-adhesive labels are applied to paper documents and fiche envelopes. Labels are produced from record information already input. Information contained on label is: SuDoc class; title (up to 80 characters); depository library announcement; item class; shipping list number; and date received.

- Consulting with local computer service providers about potential hardware needs and availability, software needs and availability, and costs
- Consulting with colleagues so that systems to be developed will interface, to the greatest extent possible, with other automation plans or activities in the library
- Doing all of the above while keeping the library director informed at each step of the way so that administrative support may be planned and expected

Conclusion

Depending on need, technology may be viewed in different ways. For regional depositories, or depositories at research libraries collecting large portions of the item classes offered by the GPO, technology is looked to primarily as an aid to finding and organizing materials. For the majority of the depository community, however, and the small to medium selective depositories that are trying to collect only those things appropriate to a particular institution and community, technology presents an opportunity not only for another means of access and control, but perhaps the only opportunity for meaningful collection development and management. Ironically, those depositories which most need the management capabilities afforded by automation are least likely to ever consider implementing such systems. These depositories are in small to medium-sized libraries that tend to have less budget flexibility and more homogeneous staffing patterns than larger libraries.

Lest the obvious still be overlooked, let me make emphatically clear that automation is only a *tool*. It, in itself, is not an end but a means to an end. It will enable documents librarians to view problems of depository collection development and management in ways substantially different from the paper past. The possibility of making a consistent and relevant connection between the relationships of item class discontinuance, rejection, deletion, and addition that govern the building and maintenance of a documents collection and the actual documents on the shelf via an automated shelflist or catalog offers a promise of effectiveness and efficiency that heretofore has been unthinkable for the documents librarian.

A *caveat* merits note: Librarians must guard against what Donald Swanson calls "the monolithic approach," the avoidance of solving anything until everything can be solved. Such thinking represents what Swanson calls the "fallacy of the ideal."[12] Too often, the promise of tomorrow's technology diverts us from the applications of today's technology. Those unwilling to philosophically or theoretically embrace today's technology will, in all probability, be equally unable or unwilling to embrace tomorrow's technology. Whatever mistakes we make today in either choosing or using technology (and we are sure to make some) should be viewed as a learning experience that will make tomorrow's technology, and our use of it, better. If we do nothing, nothing is learned; if nothing is learned, we accomplish only that which has been already accomplished. We stand in danger of allowing the past and present to become a barrier to the future. With good planning, almost any data stored via today's technology can later be electronically transferred to newer and better software and hardware. We are fortunate to be witnessing a time when the applications of this powerful technology to documents librarianship are beginning to be defined. I trust that we shall adapt to this technology just as we must learn to adjust it to our needs.

In closing, I would like to bring to the reader's attention ALA's Government Documents Round Table's Machine-Readable Government Information Task Force. I invite the reader's participation in this group as a way of continuing to educate yourself and your colleagues, of stimulating your thinking, and of contributing to the advancement of librarianship. I might also add that GODORT, in recognizing the timeliness and relevance of the issue of computer technology to documents librarianship, is offering (as one of its two programs at ALA's 1983 national convention in Los Angeles) a program titled "The Relevance of Machine-Readable Information for Gaining Access to, and Management of, Documents Collections."

References

1. Michael D. Kathman and Virgil F. Massman, *Options for the 80s: Proceedings of the Second National Conference of the Association of College and Research Libraries*, 2 vols. (Greenwich, CT: JAI Press, 1982).

2. Ruth Dahlgren Hartman, "Options for the 80s: How Does the Documents Librarian Meet the Challenges of the 80s?" *Options for the 80s: Proceedings of the Second National Conference of the Association of College and Research Libraries* (Greenwich, CT: JAI Press, 1982), pp. 519–29.

3. Ibid., p. 527.

4. Efforts (other than my own) to automate documents operations have been made by Richard Leacy at Georgia Tech, Frank Adamovich at the University of New Hampshire, Daisy Wu at the University of Wisconsin, and others. There is some talk of automation at several depositories as well.

5. Bruce Morton, "An Items Record Management System: First Step in the Automation of Collection Development in Selective GPO Depository Libraries," *Government Publications Review* 8A (1981): 193.

6. *See* Bruce Morton and J. Randolph Cox, "Cooperative Collection Development Between Selective U.S. Depository Libraries," *Government Publications Review* 9 (1982): 221–29.

7. For examples and discussion in a larger context, *see* Bruce Morton, "Implementing an Automated Shelflist for a Selective Depository Collection: Implications for Collection Management and Public Access," *Government Publications Review* 9 (1982): 332–33.

8. Superintendent of Documents, *Summary Report of Depository Libraries* (Washington, DC: U.S. Government Printing Office, October 1979, 27), indicates that 66.3 percent of depository libraries find it necessary to purchase commercial indexes in order to fully utilize depository materials.

9. Charles R. McClure, "An Integrated Approach to Government Publication Collection Development," *Government Publications Review* 8A (1981): 5.

10. *See* Bruce Morton, "Toward a Comprehensive Collection Development Policy for Partial U.S. Depository Libraries," *Government Publications Review* 7A (1980): 41–46.

11. Bruce Morton, "New Management Problems for the Documents Librarian: Government Microfiche Publications," *Microform Review* 11 (Fall 1982): 254–58.

12. Don R. Swanson, "Miracles, Microcomputers, and Librarians," *Library Journal* 107 (June 1, 1982): 1058–59.

ONLINE RETRIEVAL OF GOVERNMENT DOCUMENTS USING TELETEXT AND VIDEOTEXT SERVICES

By Susanna Schweizer

What new technology has had an impact on government documents collections? Certainly, government documents librarians do not consider online searching as new technology; after all, it has been in existence since the 1970s. Yet in looking at Charles McClure's research findings, it is apparent that online searching has not been integrated into the mainstream of documents librarianship: two-thirds of the professional documents librarians have not received training on DIALOG, ORBIT, or BRS, and the average time online per week for those who did search was about ten minutes.[1] What has caused this lag in the use of online databases by documents librarians? Perhaps one reason is the trend toward centralizing online searching within an organization or institution.

In many environments, online searching is centralized under one individual or department (usually the reference department) because of the expenses of terminals, documentation, and training. Online searching, then, *is* available in organizations, but often has been artificially separated from the many environments in which it might have been integrated into daily routine. Charles McClure's findings substantiate this centralization trend; he notes that the typical response to his queries concerning online searching in institutions was that the "other librarians do online searching."[2]

It is important to question the effectiveness of government document database searching by non-documents librarians for at least two reasons. One reason is that the idiosyncrasies of both government databases and the government documents in other databases can best be handled by those professionals specializing in a comparative print collection.[3] A second reason is the number and variety of online databases containing not only citations to government documents, but also government-generated source data. Currently, there are at least twenty-four databases (excluding patent and trademark databases) in which 50 percent of the material is federal documents,[4] and over twenty additional, publicly available databases that have a smaller percentage of government documents. To be an effective searcher of government databases, therefore, a person must keep current in about forty-four of them. This is a large number of databases with which to be familiar, especially if a person is not already acquainted with the varieties of content and format of source documents.

To summarize, then, the argument supporting documents librarians searching online for government documents is based on two points: (1) A search is best done by the person knowing the comparable print source; and (2) the number of databases containing government documents is so great that it would be difficult for a nonspecialist to keep up with them. These are two strong points, but they do not address the issue of the high cost of training, documentation, and equipment that prompted the initial centralization of the search service. Though we can argue that documents librarians should be doing the searches, we cannot easily make the system available to them because of the nature of the search system. The search system itself is one of the barriers to its own wider use; it is so detailed and cumbersome that a significant amount of training and consistent use is required for an individual not only to become and remain proficient in the necessary mechanics and skills, but also to develop the creativity and flexibility required for effective searching. Perhaps what we should be interested in is not who is doing the search, but rather the search system itself.

Criteria for an alternate search system to DIALOG, BRS or SDC include ease of use, minimal training, ease of update, cost-effectiveness, and high storage capacity. Technologies which meet these criteria and which have been receiving a great deal of attention lately are teletext and videotext.

The remainder of this chapter will discuss these technologies in general, including definitions, experiments, and the advantages and disadvantages of each. It will conclude with a discussion of the use of teletext and videotext systems in relation to the dissemination of data generated by the federal government.

Definitions

Teletext and videotext have been around less than fifteen years and, in that short time, have spawned their own terminology, a terminology in which trade names are used interchangeably with technological concepts, and clarity and consistency are rare. For example, the term videotext was used by Efrem Sigel in the title of his 1980 publication to describe "the essence of the new service—the display of textual information, both words and numbers, on a video screen."[5] In comparison, an editor's note to a 1981 article by Henry and Elizabeth Urrows defined videotext as a "generic term for two-way communication systems using the telephone network and television receivers for displays."[6] The definition in the Urrows' article is quite different from Sigel's. Recognizing the confusion both in the literature and in oral presentations, it is first necessary to present definitions.

Viewdata
Viewdata will be used as the generic term for the digital transmission of electronic pages of words and/or graphics by phone lines, cable TV lines, or broadcast TV signals to personal computers, terminals, and/or modified television receivers located in home or office. The user of the system is able to identify those electronic pages relevant to his information need by wending his way through a series of menu-type indexes. Viewdata, then, can be considered an umbrella term for various technologies used to transmit and display data.

Teletext
Teletext is one of the technologies covered by the viewdata umbrella. This technology is a one-way system of broadcasting digital data along with the usual television signal. In the United States, the television signal consists of 525 vertical lines, some of which are not used for pictorial information. These unused lines can be seen by a viewer if the horizontal hold is not adjusted properly, resulting in scrolling black bars. These black bars are technically called the vertical blanking interval. In teletext technology, data are inserted on one or more of the unused horizontal lines within the vertical interval, and these data are transmitted along with the regular broadcast. For example, PBS stations usually transmit their teletext signals over line 21. A viewer must have a decoder attached to his television in order to view the inserted data signal on his screen. The decoder itself has two functions: first, a decoder with an accompanying calculator-like keypad enables the user to select one of the 100 or so pages of data being broadcast and, second, the decoder transforms the digital signals making up the selected page into a full screen of text and/or graphics.

The width and length of an electronic page varies, but 20 characters across, and between 32 to 40 lines down, make up a typical display. The collection of pages within a system is often referred to as the electronic magazine. Sequencing through screens, then, is analogous to flipping through pages in a printed magazine. The aim of teletext is to disseminate information via a system that is easy to use and easy to update. It is basically an information retrieval service that does not require training and documentation for its use.

Teletext is considered to be a one-way transmission of data because the viewer cannot communicate with the broadcaster. When the viewer selects which screen or page of information he wants to see, he is merely indicating to the decoder which of the many broadcasted pages is to be captured from the broadcasted signal, converted, and displayed on the screen. The viewer, therefore, is not broadcasting his selection back to the television studio where the information originated. A true interaction between viewer and supplier of information occurs in the second view-data technology—videotext.

Videotext

Videotext is a two-way system in which the viewer can request information from a potentially larger collection of data. The technology of the two-way system employs either cable TV or the ubiquitous phone line. Messages are sent both to and from the viewers over one of the two communication channels, thus eliminating the dependency on the broadcast signal of teletext. The viewer uses a terminal, a personal computer (i.e., microcomputer) or a specially designed keypad to input his choices or data into the videotext system. A significant advantage of videotext over teletext is the size of the data collection at the fingertips of the viewer. In teletext the amount of information is limited to the number of pages which can be broadcast in one cycle. In videotext the number of pages is almost limitless. To clarify this difference, a short explanation of cycle time is required.

Cycle time is inherent in teletext because the data are transmitted via television signals. It is necessary to remember that television transmission is relatively continuous; if it were not so, there would be a staccato-like display of images on the screen. Since textual data are piggybacked on the regular television broadcast, the pages of information are continually being transmitted. The time it takes to broadcast the full sequence of 100 pages in the electronic magazine is called the cycle time.

Cycle time must be kept relatively short or the viewer will have to wait too long for the particular screen he has chosen. For example, in teletext, if there are 100 pages in the system "magazine," and it takes a quarter of a second to transmit each page, it would take 25 seconds for the entire sequence of pages to be broadcast. In the case where the viewer chooses a page which was just broadcast, he would have to wait another full cycle (i.e., 25 seconds) for his choice to be broadcast again and then captured and decoded for display. If the cycle is long (i.e., if the user has to wait for a long time) he will become annoyed and anxious. A balance must be achieved between the number of pages in the magazine (and, therefore, the cycle time necessary to transmit the full-sequence of pages) and the amount of time a user must wait for the screen of his choice to be displayed.

In contrast, with videotext technology, there is no cycle time which limits the maximum number of pages in the magazine. The maximum number of pages or screens a videotext system can potentially transmit is limited principally by the size of the auxiliary storage of the computer supporting the system. Hundreds, if not tens of thousands, of pages can quite easily be stored utilizing current mass storage technology. Using the keypad, communicating microcomputer, or terminal, the user simply indicates the number of the page in the electronic magazine; his page choice is transmitted to the videotext computer, and the page of the magazine is then sent to him.

The two-way nature of videotext technology not only increases the number of potential pages which can be transmitted compared to the teletext system, but also enables the system to offer transactional and interactive services in addition to the information retrieval service available in teletext. Transactional services enable the viewer to complete much of his day-to-day business while in the comfort of his home. Examples of such services include bill payment, home banking, selection and purchase of theatre tickets, making hotel and airline reservations, and electronic shopping. In contrast, the interactive services afforded by videotext are more of a two-way communication service between users of the system. Examples include electronic message centers for system subscribers, public opinion polls, real-time user-to-user communication (just like talking on a telephone except that a keyboard is used instead), and personalized education.

The remainder of this chapter will focus on the advantages and disadvantages of viewdata technology and then discuss how the agencies of the federal government are utilizing it to disseminate data. Before continuing, however, some of the current teletext and videotext systems, both operational and experimental, will be reviewed.

Current Teletext and Viewdata Projects

Teletext Projects
There are at least twelve teletext systems within the United States (see Figure 4-1).[7] Both commercial and public broadcasters are experimenting with teletext. The West Coast is the site of most of these tests, Los Angeles hosting at least three, including NBC's TEMPO, CBS's EXTRAVISION, and the local PBS's (i.e., KCET's) NOW: THE ELECTRONIC MAGAZINE. Most of these experimental projects are designed to expose the public to teletext and to evaluate the technology's appeal, as well as to enable the broadcasters to gain editorial and technical expertise. Commercial broadcasters are also investigating the commercial potential of teletext as an advertising medium. For example, KPIX in San Francisco carries between eight hundred and a thousand classified ads in one of its electronic magazines.

Figure 4-1: Teletext Services

Sponsor	Name of Service	Location
CBS (local KNXT)	Extravision	Los Angeles
Field Enterprises	Keyfax	Chicago
NBC	Tempo NBC	Los Angeles
WETA	–	Washington, D.C.
PBS (KCET)	NOW, The Electronic Magazine	Los Angeles
KPIX	Direct Vision	San Francisco
PBS (WGBH)	SCOOP	Boston
WKRC	–	Cincinnati
*Time	–	Orlando, San Diego
University of Alaska	–	Alaska
*Ottoway Newspapers	–	Danbury, CT
*Cablesystems Pacific	–	Portland, OR
*Dow Jones	Dow Jones Cable News	USA

*Cable Teletext

An illustration of a teletext service can be seen in Figure 4-2. This display contains pages from WGBH's (Boston's public broadcasting station) electronic magazine. WGBH's teletext magazine, called SCOOP, is designed as an educational news service for high school students. The teletext receivers are located in public high schools, a museum, and a department store. The first screen displayed in SCOOP shows the table of contents for the magazine. (This type of page is often called a menu.) The user of the system decides which entry in the table of contents is of interest to him and then indicates his choice by entering the corresponding page number on his keypad. The teletext system responds by displaying the chosen page. The page the user chooses may be another menu page or a page of information.

For example, look at SCOOP's table of contents in Part A of Figure 4-2. Imagine that the user was interested in the weather and selected number 43 on his keypad. Part B shows page 43, the Weather Vane page. A short forecast is given there, as well as a menu listing other weather-related pages. Part C in Figure 4-2 is the page displayed as a result of selecting page 47, the Almanac.

Though most of the teletext projects have been designed for local areas, both CBS and NBC have announced plans to initiate nationwide teletext services. CBS planned to start its service in the fall of 1982, while NBC hopes to start its service in 1983. KCET, the public television station in Los Angeles, also plans to develop a national teletext service which would be available to all PBS stations. It is projected that the magazine of these national services will be supplemented with teletext pages of local interest.

Videotext Projects

The number of videotext projects in the United States is difficult to determine because many corporations are developing in-house videotext systems, Digital Equipment Corporation and Honeywell among them. Figure 4-3 lists eleven publicly available videotext systems that are either experimental or operational. In contrast to teletext, traditional broadcasters do not have an overwhelming advantage in videotext technology because the data are sent via phone lines or cable TV. Therefore, though broadcasters such as CBS are active, other corporations are taking the initial lead.

Currently, the largest videotext system is the Dow Jones News Retrieval Service, with about 40,000 subscribers. CompuServe has about 30,000 subscribers and claims to add about 100 daily. A third service, The Source, has about 15,000 subscribers. The Source and Dow Jones' News Retrieval Service are oriented to the information needs of the business and financial worlds, while CompuServe has targeted the U.S. population in general. It is interesting to note that one of the largest users of The Source is Wheaton College, where the system is used as a reference service as well as a source of educational material, financial data, and games, and as an instrument with which to communicate with other Source users in the country.[8]

Dow Jones, CompuServe, and The Source usually limit pages of information to alphabetic and numeric characters—quite different from a typical page in the WGBH magazine above. Figure 4-4 is a display of

Figure 4-2: Pages from SCOOP Magazine (WGBH, Boston)

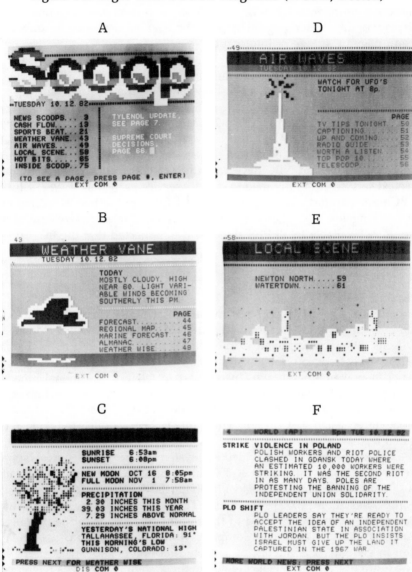

68

Figure 4-3: Videotext Services

Sponsor	Name of Service	Location
Times Mirror Company	—	California
Dow Jones	Dow Jones News Retrieval	U.S.A.
CBS	—	Ridgewood, NJ
Knight-Ridder	VIEWTRON	South Florida
First Bank Systems	FIRSTHAND	Fargo, ND
Honeywell, Inc., Centel Corp., Field Enterprises	KEYTRAN	Chicago
Radio Shack	Tandy Videotex Service (TVS)	Fort Worth, TX
Citibank	—	New York, NY
Chemical Bank	Project Pronto	New York, NY
H.R. Block	CompuServe	U.S.A.
Reader's Digest	The Source	U.S.A.

information from CompuServe. The first block in Column 1 shows CompuServe's initial system menu. The second block in Column 1 shows the menu for the Reference Library available on CompuServe. Column 2 shows the menu for the energy material available, followed by the Table of Contents for a GPO document, *Firewood for Your Fireplace*; the column ends with a display of text from the same document.

Evaluation of Viewdata Technologies

There is much debate in the literature concerning the advantages and disadvantages of teletext and videotext systems. The discussion here is meant only to be representative; it does not attempt to be comprehensive.

Advantages
Four advantages of viewdata systems are currency (ease of update), dynamic coverage, ease of use, and remote delivery of data. The first advantage, currency, is possible because these information systems can be updated immediately. In a matter of seconds, a news release from one of the wire services can be edited, entered into the system and made available to a user. The gap between the generation of the data and their transfer to those who need them is dramatically shortened. It is possible to draw the attention of users to fast-breaking stories by featuring the stories on the Table of Contents page. For example, on Part A of Figure 4-2, the editors of SCOOP made special note of the Tylenol update as well as the announcement of a Supreme Court decision.

Figure 4-4: Example of CompuServe Service*

Block 1

!T

COMPUSERVE   PAGE CIS-1

COMPUSERVE INFORMATION SERVICES

1 HOME SERVICES
2 BUSINESS & FINANCIAL
3 PERSONAL COMPUTING
4 SERVICES FOR PROFESSIONALS

5 USER INFORMATION
6 INDEX

ENTER YOUR SELECTION NUMBER,
OR H FOR MORE INFORMATION.

!

Block 2

COMPUSERVE   PAGE HOM-20

REFERENCE LIBRARY
 1 BETTER HOMES & GARDENS
 2 MOVIE REVIEWS
 3 POPULAR SCIENCE
 4 THE REFUNDLE BUNDLE
 5 U.S. GOVERNMENT PUBLICATIONS
 6 VIDEO INFORMATION
 7 THE FUTURE FILE
 8 THE VICTORY GARDEN
 9 PAN AMERICAN TRAVEL GUIDE
10 GANDOLF'S REPORT
11 HEALTH-TEX

LAST MENU PAGE. KEY DIGIT
OR M FOR PREVIOUS MENU.

!5

Block 3

COMPUSERVE   PAGE GPO-9

ENERGY CONSERVATION

1 FIREWOOD FOR YOUR FIREPLACE
2 LOW COST–NO COST ENERGY SAVERS

LAST MENU PAGE. KEY DIGIT
OR M FOR PREVIOUS MENU.

!1

COMPUSERVE   PAGE GPO-1850

FIREWOOD FOR YOUR FIREPLACE
(TABLE OF CONTENTS)

1 INTRODUCTION
2 USING WOOD IN YOUR FIREPLACE
3 WHERE TO GET FIREWOOD
4 HOW TO BUY FIREWOOD
5 BEST WOOD FOR BURNING
6 HOW TO BUILD A BETTER FIRE
7 HOW TO BUILD A SAFE FIRE

LAST MENU PAGE. KEY DIGIT
OR M FOR PREVIOUS MENU.

!5

COMPUSERVE   PAGE GPO-1831
_____
BEST WOOD FOR BURNING
_____

CHOOSING A KIND OF FIREWOOD TO
BURN IN YOUR FIREPLACE IS MUCH
LIKE SELECTING A FAVORITE WINE OR
CHEESE, SINCE EACH WOOD SPECIES
CAN OFFER SOMETHING DIFFERENT IN
AROMA OR HEAT VALUE. THE FUEL-
WOOD CONNOISSEUR WILL WANT TO
CHOOSE HIS WOOD CAREFULLY AND
WEIGH HIS NEEDS.

*Typeset from computer printed original.

As a result of ease of update, the information provider for the magazine typically does not hesitate to change, modify, or append data. There are no monthly or quarterly updates, and revised editions are unheard of because constant revision is the nature of the magazine. Ease of update, then, can eliminate the arduous tasks associated with traditional print sources, such as shuttling between volumes, yearbooks, revised editions, and/or indexes that are not cumulated.

A second advantage of viewdata systems is the dynamic coverage of an event or topic. Viewdata technology, supported by a flexible editorial policy, enables the electronic magazine to expand or contract its focus on a given issue. Again using the example of the Tylenol incident—when the scare was at its height, the number of pages devoted to use warning, recalls, and discussions of product packaging could easily have been increased immediately.

The third advantage to be discussed here is the ease of use of the system. Viewdata systems are designed to be used after little, if any, training and without the support of detailed user manuals. Typically, the nature and scope of the system are explained to users, and a brief set of instructions is supplied. An effective viewdata system is designed to lead the user cordially through the system to the needed information. Roger Phillips of Wheaton College Library reports that first-time users of The Source ". . .do not just walk [up] and try the system, but usually they will watch over someone's shoulder before jumping in themselves."[9]

Remote delivery of data is a fourth advantage of viewdata. One of the aims of viewdata services is to bring the information to the individual at the time and place he can most readily access and use it. This on-site delivery of information is an attractive characteristic of both teletext and videotext services and is a contributing factor in users' desires to install these systems in libraries, businesses, and homes. Many business people like videotext because it is a system that can be accessed from their hotel rooms using a portable terminal or microcomputer. Also, this alternative method of information delivery is especially useful for the homebound and/or handicapped.

Disadvantages
The disadvantages of viewdata center around the lack of technical standards, the sophistication of the information retrieval system, the style of the presentation of information, and the cost of the technology.

The problems resulting from the lack of technical standards have received a great deal of attention in both the press and the literature. This void is especially important for teletext technology, in which the line number used is not standard, so that different decoders are needed for each available system. The United States is the only country using information networks that does not have an applicable standard issued either by government regulation or voluntary agreement among manufacturers. A recent press article predicted that this void will be filled by either a dominant force in the industry, such as AT&T, itself setting the standards, or by a battle between competing companies eager to see their own standards adopted.[10]

Several experts in the field of information services feel that another disadvantage of viewdata services is the required level of user sophistication. John Tydeman and Lawrence Zwimpfer, whose research was funded by a National Science Foundation grant, noted that "manual, visual, and cognitive skills needed to operate even electronic keyboards and a charge-per-access time militate against the slow, the uneducated, and in general the poor."[11] Christopher Weaver, a principal of Media Technology Associates Limited, noted that videotext services do not model the real world, and also observed:

There are millions of people out there who can't read above the 8th grade level. And they are expected to go through hierarchical menu systems that will take them through five levels before they get the information they need. The people who designed these systems are not sensitive to the needs of the user.[12]

A third disadvantage of viewdata systems is the format and content of the presentation of information. The amount of information at the finger tips of the user is overwhelming, some critics labeling it "information overload." The variety and breadth of the data available, however, lack complementing depth, substance and style. Tydeman and Zwimpfer likened the nature of the available information to "...staccato assessments of complex issues, even more simplified than TV news reports."[13] This disadvantage varies from service to service, depending on the policy of the information provider. Corporations using in-house videotext systems usually provide more substance, because the scope of the information is comparatively limited.

The last disadvantage of viewdata systems to be discussed here is the cost of these systems for both the provider and the user of the service. Providers of teletext and videotext services are currently spending a great deal of money in both experiments and operations; yet there is no clear indication that these investments will produce a profitable return. An industry analysis, reported in *Educational and Instructional Television*, suggested that

...for a small- to medium-sized market, a successful videotext operation after six years will need to have a total of 60,000 subscribers to attain a 'positive flow'—this presumably after the owners of the system have invested up to $19 million.[14]

The number of subscribers a service has is critical to its existence; a view-data system without paying users would be comparable to a traditional print magazine without subscribers.

In addition to the costs the service provider must bear are the costs to the user of the system. These costs include the use fee and the expense of the equipment required to access the system. As for the use fee, it is anticipated that some of the cost can be made up by charges for either advertising on the system or the opportunity to be a vendor in a tele-shopping service.

The expense of the access equipment is a potentially more difficult one to cover. The press has noted that if either teletext or videotext service is to be successful (i.e., have a high number of subscribers), the keypad, microcomputer, or terminal needed to access the system must be made available to users of the service at a minimal cost. Various solutions to this problem have been offered: one solution is to wait for the predicted microcomputer revolution to crest, by which time the average family will have purchased a personal computer; a second solution is to make the access equipment available at a reduced rate or with special financing arrangements; and a third solution is actually to give away personal computers or keypads in the target region of the viewdata service, in hopes of enticing people to subscribe to the service. This last solution is actually being considered by Mr. Dale Reistad of Home Terminal Systems in Clearwater, Florida, as a means to lure subscribers to a videotext system soon to be implemented in the area.

Having reviewed the advantages and disadvantages of teletext and videotext systems, this chapter concludes with a discussion of the federal government's involvement with these technologies.

The Federal Government and Viewdata

Projects
There is no coordinated federal effort to disseminate government-generated data via any of the teletext or videotext systems, but several departments or agencies have independently begun to offer data free of charge to viewdata systems. An informal survey, conducted by this author, of some federal departments revealed that the State Department, the Internal Revenue Service, the Department of Agriculture and the National Oceanic and Atmospheric Administration have been, or are about to be, involved in teletext and/or videotext projects.

One of the earliest videotext projects in which the federal government was involved was the Green Thumb experiment sponsored by the

Department of Agriculture (USDA) in two Kentucky counties from March 1980 to July 1981. The Green Thumb experiment which included two hundred users, offered grain and livestock data from the Chicago exchanges; local, regional, and national weather reports; and crop and livestock production information.[15-16]

Though the Green Thumb experiment has ended, commercial video-text systems are similarly disseminating USDA data. One such service is Farm News Express, which supplies USDA farm and wholesale produce reports. Initially, the price information in these reports was mailed daily as part of the USDA Market News Service, but, by the time the mailing was received, the prices were a week old. Now the information is available immediately and at a relatively reasonable cost. It is noteworthy that the Farm News Express is a private videotext service made available on CompuServe.

A second government agency actively providing information to tele-text and videotext services is the Internal Revenue Service. According to Dianne Spencer, an IRS employee responsible for disseminating tax information to various viewdata projects around the country, the IRS sees its current activity as preparatory, so that when viewdata becomes a major industry, the IRS will already have had experience with it. The type of data currently being distributed is short tips on tax law and procedure, such as how many deductions may be legally taken, or whether or not students have to file tax returns. The IRS data service has been very well received.

The State Department has plans to offer a service comparable to that of the IRS. The service would supply travel warnings and advisories to at least one national videotext system. Typical tips would include a list of countries one can only enter on a Sunday or of those countries where it is strongly advisable to refrain from wearing a backpack.

Benefits

Viewdata systems offer the federal government an opportunity to dis-seminate data via a system that is easy to use and has the potential of being available in many homes and businesses. Viewdata has fewer barriers to its use than the online systems (such as BRS, DIALOG, or ORBIT) currently used for searching government documents. The biggest advantage of viewdata is the absence of a retrieval language to master.

Teletext and videotext technologies also enable federal agencies to provide better information service to a wider group at a potentially lower cost. With the rising cost of printing, mailing, and storing printed mate-rial, viewdata can be a cost-effective technology which could easily handle all three of the above functions. The cost-saving benefits of tele-text and videotext are especially important in this era of budgetary restraint.

Conclusion

Viewdata systems provide for ease of use and update, dynamic coverage, and remote delivery of information. These advantages can be directly applied to the work of those people producing, handling, and disseminating government documents:

- Instant update can eliminate the need to cope with the currency of printed materials and the problem of tracking superseded documents.
- Ease of use and the small amount of training required increases the likelihood of all documents librarians doing online searches of the documents with which they are familiar.
- Remote delivery will enable data generated by the federal government to be transmitted directly to many of the people who need the information, at the location where it is needed.

References

1. Charles R. McClure, "Online Government Documents Data Base Searching and the Use of Microfiche Documents Online by Academic and Public Depository Librarians," *Microform Review* 10 (Fall 1981): 245–59.

2. Ibid., p. 251.

3. Ann VanCamp, "Effective Search Analysts," *Online* 3 (April 1979): 19.

4. Deborah S. Hunt, "Accessing Federal Government Documents Online," *Database* (February 1982): 10–17.

5. Efrem Sigel, *Videotext: The Coming Revolution in Home/Office Information Retrieval* (White Plains, NY: Knowledge Industry Pubns., 1980), p. 3 (unnumbered).

6. Henry and Elizabeth Urrows, "Can Videotext Work?" *Microcomputing* 5 (October 1981): 68.

7. Joseph Roizen, "Teletext—A Service That's Coming of Age," *Educational and Industrial Television* 14 (September 1982): 39.

8. Roger Phillips, "A Public Access Videotext Library Service," *Online* 6 (September 1982): 34–37.

9. Ibid., pp. 35–36.

10. Kathryn Jones, "Lack of Net Standards Scored," *MIS Week* 3 (December 8, 1982): 25.

11. Urrows, "Can Videotext Work?" p. 75.

12. Henry Weiss, "Problems with Videotex: Still Too Smart for Some Users," *MIS Week* (March 28, 1982), p. 26.

13. Urrows, "Can Videotext Work?" p. 75.

14. Charles S. Tepfer, "Keeping Up with Videotex," *Educational and Instructional Television* 14 (September 1982): 36.

15. "FNE Operates as Private Videotex System," *Today* (July/August 1982): 14–15.

16. Donald Case et al., *Standford Evaluation of the Green Thumb Box Experimental Videotext Project for Agricultural Extension Information Delivery in Shelby and Todd Counties, Kentucky* (Springfield, VA: National Technical Information Service, 1981), PB82-190281.

NEW TECHNOLOGY
AND STATE GOVERNMENT
INFORMATION SOURCES

By Terry L. Weech

Until recently, state government information sources have been
considered in terms of three categories: published government documents, archival records, and personal knowledge of state government
staff. Libraries, archives, and government staff contacts have often been
the means of gaining access to these three sources of information. New
technology is bringing about some significant changes in how we
approach these traditional sources and is also establishing some new
sources for state government information. Electronic data processing
(EDP) technology has been the catalyst. Data storage and retrieval,
computer output microforms (COM), and word processing capabilities
have all affected access to state government information. Telecommunications and videorecording technology have also influenced the way
such information is packaged. The printed report, the archival record, or
the recollection of a staff member of state government on a legislative
hearing are no longer the only sources that may be available. The text of
the legislative hearing may be available in a computer memory, and the
actual proceeding may be preserved on audio or videotape. Through
telecommunications, nearly instantaneous access to these and other
sources may be available far from the center of state government. The

new technology also permits information to be revised and manipulated several times before it is preserved as a permanent record or transmitted. Electronically formulated information may be less accessible to some users than print and archival records. This chapter will discuss the use of new technology both to record state government information and to control and provide access to traditional and nontraditional government information sources. The impact of the new technology on access to state government information and the public's right to know will also be examined, with some specific recommendations regarding the preservation of that right.

New Technology and Its Impact on Traditional Sources— Printed Documents

Printed government information sources exist for every branch of state government. The executive branches usually issue the greatest volume and variety of printed publications. These publications range from annual administrative reports to handbooks, manuals and instructional brochures associated with the executive agencies' missions (e.g., "Rules of the Road" manuals for automobile drivers, or health and welfare pamphlets on good nutrition). The legislative branches of state government have, in most states, produced considerably fewer publications than the executive branches of the state or their legislative counterparts in the federal government. In most states, legislative journals, bills, and session laws make up the bulk of legislative publications. Although some state legislatures have issued printed texts of hearings and committee reports, they are the exceptions to the rule. Very few states attempt anything like the federal *Congressional Record* or the large number of publications that constitute a legislative history of a federal law.

The judicial branches of state government are probably the most limited publishers of printed information. Although some states still publish "official editions" of their reports, their judicial branches seem to be relying more and more on commercially published sources such as West's *National Reporter System* for court decisions.

Access to these traditional sources has usually been through printed catalogs, indexes, or checklists. The only ongoing national attempt at bibliographic control is the Library of Congress's *Monthly Checklist of State Publications*. The value and limitations of this tool are well known by all who have used it. Although there are many gaping holes in the bibliographic net that the *Checklist* attempts to throw over state publications, it is the best we presently have at the national level. Another attempt to provide access to state government information was Information Handling Services' *State Publication Index*, which was discontinued in 1981. Most states have developed their own checklists for their printed publications. These checklists are often used by those wanting to verify printed information sources from a specific state. But many of the checklists are less than complete in their coverage, and the indexing and production schedules often leave much to be desired.

In an attempt to improve access, several applications of new technology to the bibliographic control of printed state information sources have been made. Over half of the states input their publications into an online bibliographic network. OCLC is by far the most commonly used network. As of 1980, twenty-four state publication depository agencies in twenty-four states indicated that they input into OCLC most or all of their state publications received on deposit. Three states were either inputting, or planning to input, into WLN. California indicated it was inputting into RLIN.[1]

One of the benefits, of course, of inputting state government information sources into a regional or national online bibliographic network is that the holdings of member libraries can be shared. The potential "union listing," which would provide physical access to the publications through the nearest depository, has not materialized to the extent some had hoped. One study in Illinois of 252 state publications distributed to Illinois state depository libraries in the fourth quarter of 1980 revealed that depositories which were also members of the OCLC network failed to input state government publication holding information from most of the depository publications they received. Excluding the Illinois State Library, the twenty-two depositories that were also OCLC members indicated holding symbols in OCLC for less than half of the state publications received. The median number for which holdings were indicated was five (2 percent of the total). Twenty-three percent of the depositories did not input any of the state publications they received. The best effort of the twenty-two depositories was the one library that input 48 percent of the depository publications.[2] A sample of fifty-two publications sent a year earlier to the Illinois depositories yields a slightly better result, but is still far short of the input necessary for a true union listing. The range for the 1979 data was from 0 percent to 69 percent entered into the OCLC database, with a median at three of the fifty-two titles entered.[3] There are, of course, many factors that may explain why such a low percentage of Illinois state depository publications are input into the bibliographic network, including a variety of policies relating to cataloging and classification of state government publications in each library. But one of the promises of the new technology—access to government publications through an online union listing—seems not to have been realized in Illinois. Information on the success or failure of other states in this regard could not be found in the literature.

The OCLC bibliographic record is also used in several states to generate checklists. Kansas, one of the first states to develop a program to generate a state checklist of publications from OCLC tapes, has offered the program to other states. At least three states—Iowa, Louisiana, and Utah—are now using, or are planning on using, the Kansas program to produce catalogs or checklists of their publications.[4] Computer output microform (COM) has been used by at least one state to generate state publication checklists.[5] Texas is reported to be developing an online database of its publications called TEXDOC, which will produce the printed *Texas State Documents Checklist* and provide online subject access. Undoubtedly, as more state depository agencies gain access to computers, more computer generated catalogs and checklists, as well as greater online subject access, will result.

Although it may not be considered a new technology so much as a technological alternative to printing, the use of microforms (other than COM) will be commented on briefly. More and more states are distributing most or all of their publications to depository libraries in microformat, usually microfiche. Nebraska, which was one of the first states to distribute microfiche publications to depositories, is now distributing its publications *checklist* exclusively in microfiche as well.[6] Cost and ease of duplication are usually factors in the decision to substitute microforms for printed copies. The utilization of COM and other computer technology promises even greater use of microfiche for state government information in the future.

New Technology and New Sources

When it comes to the impact of new technology on sources of information, the legislative branch of state government has been the most visible. The Library of Congress's Congressional Research Service conducted a study of state legislatures' use of new information technology, the results of which were published in 1977.[7] The ten major applications of new technology by state legislatures that were identified include
- Bill content and status
- Bill drafting
- Statutory retrieval
- Photocomposition
- Electronic voting
- Fiscal/budgetary control
- Computerized modeling
- Audio/video technology

- Political redistricting
- Administration

Comparing three functions for which data are available over an eight-year period, bill drafting has had the greatest increase in the number of states adopting electronic data processing (EDP) technology. Table 5-1 provides comparative data.

Table 5-1: EDP in State Legislatures

	1972		1980	
	Operating	Planned	Operating	Planned
Bill Drafting	11	18	34	2
Status of Legislation	25	10	40	1
Statutory Retrieval	25	11	35	

[1972 data from U.S. Library of Congress, Science Policy Research Division, *State Legislature Use of Information Technology* (Washington: GPO, 1977), p. 26. 1980 data from *Book of the States, 1980–81* (Lexington, KY: Council of State Governments, 1980), Table 33, pp. 138–39.]

As of 1980, the use of EDP information systems to determine the status of bills is the most widespread application; but bill drafting and other applications are rapidly catching up. The report of the Congressional Research Service points out that those state legislatures which were first involved with electro-mechanical or electronic voting devices (the first application of information technology by most state legislatures) were usually among the first to adopt other information technology systems.[8] As states have success with bill status information systems, adoption of other information systems should occur as rapidly as funds and technology permit.

Another technology that has had an impact on the legislative branch is that of audio and video recordings. There is no indication in the literature of the number of legislatures that broadcast their proceedings on radio, but at least twenty-three states make audio recordings of some or all of their legislative hearings available.[9] Most states permit television coverage of their legislative sessions. Although there seems to be nothing comparable to the coverage of the U.S. House of Representatives, a number of public television networks provide fairly thorough coverage of state legislative deliberations.[10-11]

The judicial branches of state governments have made some use of EDP information systems in the management and administration of court business. Computers have mostly been used for compiling statistical data and budgetary reports. They have also been used to select the names of jurors in over two hundred courts in the United States. Twenty-three states have participated in the State-Centered Judicial Information System (SJIS), with the support of the Federal Law Enforcement Assistance Administration, since it was established in the 1970s. There have been criticisms of the SJIS system, however, for its concentration on criminal data when in fact most state courts deal with noncriminal cases.[12] Another program funded by the Federal Law Enforcement Assistance Administration is the Prosecutor's Management Information System (PROMIS). Some courts have expanded the system to include general management and record-keeping functions so that general trial courts can use the system as a state central court management device.[13]

Television, along with videorecording, is a technology which has been utilized by some state courts. Although still a controversial issue, more and more states seem to be considering granting permission for videorecordings of court proceedings. As of 1981, thirty-one states allowed television coverage of judicial proceedings.[14]

The executive branches *seem* to be lagging behind in the application of new technologies. But this appearance may be deceptive. Most of the executive branches of the states utilize computers in some areas of directory and numeric data compilation; the use of electronic data processing to maintain lists of motor vehicle registrations, driver's license data, and members of certified and licensed occupations, are some of the early examples. Tax data, state budget data, school, library, health, and other statistical data are included in the numeric databases maintained by the state executive agencies. There appears to be some consistency from state to state in what is input in an online format, but as the microcomputer becomes more readily available in state executive branch agencies, the amount of state government information accessible through it will undoubtedly grow.

Access to the New Sources

Access to the electronic information systems of state legislatures is generally limited to the members of the legislatures and their staffs. Indirect access can sometimes be gained by telephoning legislative information offices or other state agencies that have direct access to the legislative information system. Some states provide toll-free 800 numbers for access to legislative bill status information. Several commercial vendors are now offering access to information on legislation at the state level. The commercial systems include *Legislate*, PAIS's *Public Affairs Information*, and Commerce Clearing House's *Electronic Legislative Search*

System. Such systems provide (or will provide when fully operational) access to information on bill status and other legislative activities in all fifty states. The present pattern seems to be to make state legislative information systems directly available to persons outside the legislatures through commercial services only.

The audio recordings of state legislative hearings and proceedings are often even less readily available than computer-based systems. Such recordings are usually thought of as "archival" records and are thus not widely distributed. Some states make audio tapes of legislative hearings available to libraries from a central source such as the state archives or legislative reference service, but many leave the distribution of recordings up to individual committees.[15]

Most state online systems used by judicial branches of state government are not publicly available. Commercial vendors (most notably, Westlaw and LEXIS) provide online access to some judicial activities. Information on the accessibility of court videorecordings is not available, but one might reasonably assume that such recordings are not accessible to the public.

Access to information sources produced by the executive branches of state governments through new technological means remains the most elusive. Most of the directory and numeric data compiled by state executive agencies are not available through public or commercial vendors. The only exceptions are those released by the state agencies in printed format that are subsequently indexed by one of the commercially vended databases such as the *Statistical Reference Index* (SRI). The information in state data archives remains out of potential users' reach.

It is evident from the above that new technologies have been utilized by state government to control and generate numerous state government information sources, but that access to these sources varies considerably. On the whole, the sources based on new technology are even less accessible to the public than those in traditional print formats. Of course, much of the information available as a result of the new technology was not available in traditional formats. The new technology has made state government information more accessible to most state government staff. But the question of the state's responsibility to make this information available to the public must be raised. Insofar as much of current access is through commercial rather than public sources, the question of the public's right of access to governmental information would seem to be based on the principle that the public has a right to information that the private sector finds commercially profitable. At present we seem to be in the middle of an information gap in which governments have more and more access to information, but the people they govern are given less and less. What happens in the future may depend upon the success of commercial vendors and the philosophy of public access held by state government officials. This author hopes it would also depend on the ability of dedicated information professionals to maintain public access to state information sources. It is in the spirit of that hope that the following discussion is undertaken.

Freedom of Information Concerns

The use of new technology by government documents librarians is not encouraging. For whatever reasons, surveys confirm that state as well as federal government publication librarians make little use of online sources to support their reference services.[16-17] When this disuse of information in the new formats is coupled with the trend toward less public dissemination of government information, the concern over access to information becomes critical. This concern has been expressed by the documents librarians working on the American Library Association's GODORT State and Local Documents Task Force. The Task Force has established a Freedom of Information Committee to determine, among other things, the extent to which public access to information in online formats is limited. Bills of state legislatures are provided when online revision in status is substituted for printed documents.[18] But the concern cannot be limited to legislative information. We must also be concerned over the lack of access to numeric data at the state level. Kathleen Heim, for one, presented a paper at the Second Annual Library Government Documents and Information Conference which focused on access to federal numeric data archives.[19] But with many state agencies developing numeric databases in small, decentralized computers, access to these data may be even more limited. Gary Purcell, in a recent survey of reference services relating to state government information, found that 73 of the 113 libraries responding to the survey (64 percent) indicated that they did not provide services relating to state level numeric databases.[20] Only 37 respondents indicated that they would refer users to agencies that provided access to numeric databases. There would seem to be real resistance to referring inquirers to agencies that can provide access to such numeric information.

The National Association of State Information Systems (NASIS) has expressed a similar concern from a different perspective. One of the primary concerns expressed by NASIS's members is the need for co-ordination and control as a result of the proliferation of data processing equipment and personnel in state government. NASIS cites the more than doubling of the number of minicomputers installed from 1972 to 1978 (70 to 171) and the growth of mini's from 2 percent of the total number of computers in 1973 to 24 percent in 1978.[21] No data could be found on the impact of microcomputers on state government electronic data processing installations, but it is unlikely that the trend toward distributed systems has been decreased with their greater availability. NASIS's concern is with the security and standardization of programs and databases as well as operational efficiency. This is not much different from the concern of librarians and information scientists with access to information. Clearly the time is approaching when we must ensure public access to state information stored in electronic as well as print sources. The following proposal is one possible direction.

Government Information Specialists—A Blending of Professions

At the present time, archivists, documents librarians, and information systems administrators are working on various aspects of the problem of storing and retrieving state government information. It is proposed that a blending of the concerns of all these professionals for the access and control of state government information be considered. In no way is it suggested here that the archivists', documents librarians', or information systems administrators' positions be done away with. Rather, each of the institutions that today support these professionals could benefit from a team member trained to be sensitive to the concerns of all the professions involved in state government information processing and capable of communicating across institutional and professional boundaries to achieve the goal of public access and information preservation. The need for an intermediary between government information source and user will increase as both the information itself and the sources that state governments produce become more complex. Even if every home is equipped with the technology to access online state information, someone must be certain that the information is accessible to such systems and that it is frozen at appropriate intervals to provide accurate records of government operations. Otherwise we are in danger of a constant revision not only of our past but of our present, and we will have only a semblance of accountability on the part of government officials. It may be time for the librarian, playing the role of the traffic cop of information (as envisaged by Ortega y Gasset over forty years ago), to come to the forefront in the guise of a specialist dealing with government information access.

This new professional might be called a "government information specialist." His/her concerns would not be limited to one level of government, since all levels interact and influence each other. Knowledge of federal, state, and local government information sources would be necessary. This specialist would be instilled with the commitment of the archivist to preserving materials, the commitment of the documents librarian to information dissemination, and the skills of the information system administrator.

One way to ensure that this specialist is appropriately trained is to provide a formal study curriculum. It might be part of a six-year specialist degree, drawing students from a master's program in library and information science, computer science, political science, public administration, history, and other related disciplines. It would have to be a flexible, interdisciplinary curriculum, providing primary courses to build on the student's strengths and supplementary courses to correct his deficiencies. Such a specialist would, in my opinion, be the first step toward ensuring that state government information—in whatever form and produced by whatever technology—would be preserved and made available for the present and future constituents of state governments. Without this protection, I think we need to be concerned about the tradition of the informed press and the informed public in an open and free society. I am not suggesting that there is presently any intent to deprive the public of its right to access, but as states look for more ways to control costs and promote efficiency in government, it is easy to forget the long-standing commitment to freedom of access to information—especially at the state and local levels, where the press and other media are not always as watchful as they are at the national level. As valuable as commercial vendors are in the development of information dissemination systems, we must be concerned when the marketplace determines what the public will know. While it may be appropriate to let the marketplace determine what we will view or read for entertainment or purchase for consumption, it is *not* appropriate to let the marketplace determine what we can know about our government. As states take on more responsibilities under the "New Federalism," it is especially important that state government information be available to all. In my opinion, that can best be done by having a committed group of professionals working to maintain public access to government information sources, whether it be ensuring access to the text of bills deliberated by state legislatures or the numeric data on state government expenditures for public improvements. Someone must ensure that the public's right to know is maintained, and the time may have come for a specific government information specialist to provide that protection.

References

1. Yuri Nakata and Karen Kopec, "State and Local Government Publications," *Drexel Library Quarterly* 16 (October 1980): 48.

2. Ronald Winner and Sherwood, Kirk, "Illinois Document Depository Libraries' Use of OCLC Cataloging for the Depository Collection: A Survey with Implications for Revision of the Depository Program," mimeographed (Springfield, IL: Illinois State Library, 1981), p. A-17, Table 8.

3. Ibid., p. A-15, Table 6.

4. Bruce L. Flanders, "State Documents in Kansas Automated Bibliographic Control," *Documents to the People* 8 (May 1980): 114.

5. Margaret T. Lane, "Scattered Notes on State Publications," *Documents to the People* 9 (September 1981): 186.

6. Ibid.

7. U.S. Library of Congress, Science Policy and Research Division, *State Legislative Use of Information Technology* (Westport, CT: Greenwood Press, 1978). Reprint of: U.S., Congress, House, *State Legislative...*, 95th Cong., 1st Sess., 1977, H. Doc. 95-271.

8. Ibid., p. 19.

9. Mary L. Fisher, *Guide to State Legislature Materials*, American Association of Law Libraries Publication Number 15 (Littleton, CO: Rothman, 1979).

10. "State Governments Take on New Vigor," *U.S. News and World Report* (March 20, 1978): 39-40, 42-43.

11. Library of Congress, *State Legislative Use of Information Technology*, p. 143.

12. Norbert A. Halloran, "Computers in Court Administration," in *Computers and the Law*, ed. R. P. Bigelow, 3rd ed. (Chicago: Commerce Clearing House, 1981), p. 102.

13. Ibid., p. 106.

14. "Cameras in the Courts," *The News Media and the Law* 5 (October-November 1981): 64.

15. Fisher, *Guide to State Legislature Materials*.

16. Barbara Ford and Yuri Nakata, "Reference Use of State Government Information in Academic Libraries," *Government Publications Review* 10 (1983), in press.

17. Gary R. Purcell, "Reference Use of State Government Publications in Public Libraries," *Government Publications Review* 10 (1983), in press.

18. "S&LDTF Business Meeting," *Documents to the People* 10 (May 1982): 112.

19. Kathleen M. Heim, "Government Produced Machine-Readable Statistical Data as a Component of the Social Science Information System: An Examination of Federal Policy and Strategies for Access," in *Communicating Public Access to Government Information. Proceedings of the Second Annual Government Documents and Information Conference*, ed. Peter Hernon (Westport, CT: Meckler Publishing, 1983).

20. Purcell, "Reference Use of State Government Publications in Public Libraries."

21. Carl W. Vorlander, "State Information Systems," in *Book of the States, 1980-81* (Lexington, KY: Council of State Governments, 1980), p. 222, Table B.

CODOC IN THE 1980s: KEEPING PACE WITH MODERN TECHNOLOGY

By Virginia Gillham

The consensus among current authors and speakers seems to be that government document librarians have been slow to take advantage of computer technology to process their collections and provide in-depth access for their users. Furthermore, in the United States, most discussions of computer applications for these purposes are confined almost exclusively to federal government publications and the current full cataloging of them made available by the U.S. Government Printing Office.

What are American libraries doing with state and municipal documents, documents from foreign countries, and documents produced by such international organizations as the United Nations or the European Communities? Are they kept in separate collections? Are they not processed at all? What happens to the library user who wants to conduct a subject search of the output of several countries? Does he find what he needs? Does he ever come back?

The reasons for not applying traditional manual cataloging to official publications—cost, manpower, volume, and transitory value—are applicable to documents produced by the G.P.O. or other government publishers. The overriding consideration should be to provide the user with fast, painless, effective access to an entire document collection from all sources, countries, and levels of government. Surely what is really needed is one system which will handle all documents from any source with equal speed, economy, and efficiency. The result should be one comprehensive access tool for the entire collection which offers access by (among other things) author, title, and subject, and provides records that can be integrated with traditionally cataloged records in either batch or online modes.

This problem was addressed at the University of Guelph (Ontario, Canada) as long ago as 1965. The initial result was a simple batch system which was used in-house to provide catalog-type access to one institution's government documents collection. The initial design was, however, flexible enough to allow the system to be modified for batch consortium use. Later, as library systems technology became more sophisticated, the original design was adapted for online use in individual libraries and distributed networks, and it is presently part of the iNET™ field trial.[1]

This chapter will explain the basic philosophy of the original (1965) batch system, and then will give an expanded explanation of the various modifications facilitated by developing technology.

The Guelph Document System, as it was originally known, was designed to provide quick, economical, in-depth access to individual documents of any government at any level of any country. Economy is achieved partly by the processing speed which automation provides, and partly because the coding can (and should) be done by clerical staff. In the batch version of the system, coders begin with the document in hand and a blank coding form (see Figure 6-1). A code, which becomes the call number, is created, based on corporate author. It is merely a location device whose component parts represent the various factors used to arrive at a shelf location. Documents are shelved in alphabetical order first by country of origin, beginning, probably, with Albania and ending with Zambia, or whatever may be appropriate to the collection under consideration. The first two characters of the code are alphabetical and represent the country; thus, AB for Albania, CA for Canada, US for the United States, and ZM for Zambia.

Within each country, publications are arranged by level of government. Federal publications come first, followed by state or provincial where appropriate, county or regional, municipal, and so on. A single numeric character in the code identifies the level of government. All U.S. federal document codes begin with US1, state documents with US2, county with US3. Where necessary, a two-character alpha code explains the preceding numeric. US2IL is the code for Illinois and CA2ON for Ontario. Anyone with a grasp of the basic method can devise appropriate codes for areas not already designated by previous users of the system.

The next six characters of the code are used for the organization and sub-organization, usually the government department and its branches. The first three of these six characters are alphabetical and left justified,

Figure 6-1: Computer Information Coding Sheet

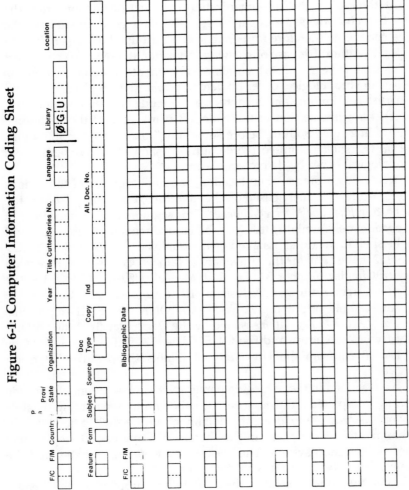

representing the main organization or department. The second three, which are right justified and numeric, are used for the sub-organization or branch. Thus, CA2ONAF 19 is the code for the Dairy Branch (19) of the Ministry of Agriculture and Food (AF) in the province of Ontario. US2ILU 40 is for the University of Illinois (U) Cooperative Extension Service (40).

At the end of the sub-organization code, all documents from the same branch of the same department of the same government have the same code. One therefore finds publications grouped on the shelves by corporate author. For ease of shelving thereafter, the next two characters are a numeric year code which allows documents to be located on the shelves in chronological order by date of publication. Serials, which are by nature continuous (and for which a year code is, therefore, inappropriate), have this section of the code left blank. Use of the traditional library filing rule "nothing before something" places serial publications first on the shelf within corporate author, followed by monographs in chronological order by date of publication.

To identify a precise shelf location, the final segment of the code is a cutter number, usually based on the title; thus, CA1EB 320-77B35 is the publication *Buds and Marine Mammals*. This segment may be used instead to repeat series numbers, to allow the components of a series to stand on the shelf in the order assigned by the publisher. For example, US2ILU 40-19C32 is the code for the University of Illinois, Cooperative Extension Service Circular number 32, *Pig Club Manual*. US2ILU 40-19C33 is the code for Circular number 33, *Fashion – Its Use and Abuse*.

An example of a complete code – CA2ONAF 19-66D11 – represents *The Dairy Acts and Regulations* issued by the Dairy Branch of the Ontario Ministry of Agriculture and Food. US2ILU 40-72C59 is the code for *Care for Your Trees*, from the University of Illinois Cooperative Extension Service.

As described in the preceding paragraphs, each segment of the code is easily interpreted. A user, however, needs no understanding whatsoever of the structure to locate the document on the shelf. Shelving is in alphanumeric sequence, as in the Library of Congress, Dewey, or any other classification system. The user who knows the alphabet and the numbers to 1,000 can find what he seeks.

After the code is created, other data are supplied in the header record, and detailed bibliographic information is entered into the body of the form (see Figure 6-2).

The document can then be labelled and sent immediately to the shelves, even before the coding information is input to disk or tape. The result of the inputting is a master file of records from which a regular set of catalog or specialized lists can be created at any time. Subject-type

Figure 6-2: Completed Computer Information Coding Sheet

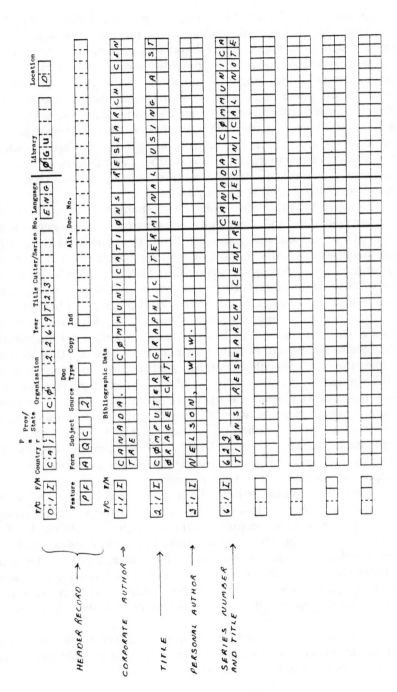

access is provided by a KWOC index produced from an enriched title file. Users have complete flexibility *vis-a-vis* title enrichment, which may be as simple or elaborate as need and staff constraints dictate.

A standard set of catalogs provides access by corporate author, personal author, title, series title, serial title, and keyword. These can be produced on paper or microform, as frequently or infrequently as the library chooses and feels it can afford to. Since inputting is in a batch mode in this version of the system, batches of data must be merged with the main file at regular intervals. Updates to the catalog are provided as a byproduct of this exercise. A typical procedure might be to produce a completely new set of catalogs two, three, or four times a year, and to supplement them with weekly updates.

As interest in this system grew, it was shared with most of the other academic libraries in Ontario, and a batch merging of files began to take place at intervals to form a union list. It was this batch consortium which originally acquired the name CODOC, by which the system is now generally known. Any library using the CODOC system is using a version of the original Guelph Document system. In addition, it may or may not be involved in consortium sharing with other user libraries.

From the beginning, members of the Ontario Consortium merged their records on a bimonthly basis and had the ability to extract records from the union file (rather than code them themselves), if they identified a match on the file with an unprocessed title in their own collection. These bimonthly merges continue today. The resulting union file of the holdings of eleven libraries is produced on microfiche for the contributors and anyone else who wishes to purchase the file. It is also mounted, online, on two Canadian database services.[2] Both services are comparable to BRS, ORBIT or DIALOGUE in the type of access they offer. In an individual library, inputting can be either batch or online, and output can be paper, microform or online.

The batch versions of both the in-house and consortium systems continue to exist, principally for the benefit of those smaller libraries which do not have the computer facilities to support anything else. Even a library with no on-site systems capabilities could code manually and then employ an off-site service agency to input and produce tapes and catalogs. Developments in automation in the past ten years, however, have created a whole range of other possibilities, and there are libraries using this system which avail themselves of just about every one of them.

Coded document records can be integrated with traditionally coded records in one of several ways in order to obviate the problem of having to remember to use two access tools. For example:

(a) Conversion programs have been used in some libraries to convert retrospective databases to MARC-compatible format to facilitate merging.

(b) Inputting parameters have been modified slightly in some libraries to yield MARC-compatible records. In these cases, conversion programs usually exist to put the data back into true CODOC format, if libraries wish to merge their records with those of other CODOC institutions.

(c) Some online systems will accept both LC and CODOC records without conversion and present to the user what appears to be a single integrated file. This is the situation at the University of Guelph, where no conversion or augmenting of coded records has been applied, although both types of records are accessible in a single online system. The user conducts only one search, and never knows he is dealing with two files.

The CODOC system is extremely flexible, allowing the content of the various fields to be modified to describe a variety of materials. As a result, it has been adapted for use with such resources as slides, phonograph records,[3] serials,[4] and archive collections.[5]

The system has been acquired by many libraries other than those in the Ontario academic group. Some have acquired the complete system, while others (usually smaller institutions) have chosen to engage in a third party agreement (a big brother/little brother relationship with a larger library which mounts the complete system).

Libraries which acquire the complete system have the opportunity to establish the nucleus of their database quickly by extracting records that match their own holdings from the Ontario union database, which presently numbers in excess of 500,000 titles. Libraries which choose the third party agreement would extract records from their parent institution in the same way.

Many libraries use this system without being part of the Ontario Consortium. Some use it independently. Others have developed small sharing groups of their own. Such groups presently exist in at least two provinces outside Ontario, and in one state.

The Ontario group considered, at length, the option of moving to a traditional star online network, but ultimately rejected it as being too expensive and headed for obsolescence. Star networks with huge union databases at their centers are expensive because they demand a large measure of conformity (and, thus, of extra staff time) and participants must pay twice to store their records both at home and with the network.

The alternative chosen by the Ontario consortium is a distributed network wherein members mount their records online at home and dial into one another's databases. There is no costly double storage of records and no pressure for unrealistic conformity. About half of the members of the Ontario group are now in a position to participate in such a network. All eleven members continue to contribute to the batch consortium, which sooner or later will probably disappear. Simultaneously, those equipped to do so have dial access to each other's holdings in a distributed network. Several users are also involved in the iNet™ field trial.

It has been said that we should not use the anticipation of tomorrow's technology as an excuse not to do something today. The activity surrounding the CODOC system in the past fifteen years demonstrates the validity of that statement. What started as a simple batch system to solve a problem in one library was adapted for consortium use, for use with semi-online and online technology, for use with other kinds of resources, and now as part of iNET™, the online experiment in database technology which represents the most exciting telecommunications phenomenon to appear to date.

References

1. "The iNET Gateway™ is an intelligent network concept developed by CCG, the Computer Communications Group of the Trans Canada Telephone System (160 Elgin St., Ottawa, Canada; tel.: 613–239–4254). The concept has evolved in recognition of the requirement for more universal accessibility to information providers and other computer-based services."

2. Can OLE is a Canadian government-sponsored on-line bibliographic information service mounted by the National Research Council of Canada. Passwords are presently available only to residents of Canada.

QL Systems is a privately operated on-line bibliographic information service which is accessible from outside Canada (1020 Vanguard Bldg., 171 Slater St., Ottawa, Canada, K1A OS9).

3. Sandra Faull, "The Codoc System at Stockton State College," Unpublished paper (Pomona, NJ: Stockton State College Library, 1976).

4. Ibid.

5. Nancy Sadek, "Codoc for an Archive," *Canadian Library Journal* 39 (1982): 75–78.

Bibliography of Publications Relating to the Codoc/Guelph Document System

1. Beckman, Margaret. "A Documentation Centre at the University of Guelph Library." *Ontario Library Reviews* 50 (1966): 226–29.

2. _____. "Documentation System for the Organization of Government Publications within a University Library." Research Report No. 2. Guelph, Ontario: University of Guelph Library, 1969.

3. _____; Henderson, Sara; and Pearson, Ellen. "The Guelph Document System." Report No. 3. Guelph, Ontario: University of Guelph Library, 1973.

4. _____, and Pearson, Ellen. "Co-operative Use of the Guelph Document System." Guelph, Ontario: University of Guelph Library, 1974. A study done for the National Library by the University of Western Ontario and the University of Guelph in co-operation with the Library of the Department of External Affairs in Ottawa.

5. *CODOC Coding Manual*. Toronto: Office of Library Co-ordination, Council of Ontario Universities, May 1976.

6. Faull, Sandra. "The Codoc System at Stockton State College." Unpublished paper. Pomona, NJ: Stockton State College Library, 1976.

7. Gillham, Virginia. "CODOC, A Canadian System for Processing Government Publications." Paper presented to the Official Publications section of I.F.L.A., Montreal, Canada, August 24, 1982.

8. _____. "Codoc as a Consortium Tool." *Government Publications Review* 9 (1982): 45-53.

9. _____. "The Guelph Document System." *Government Publications Review* 7 (1980): 211-16.

10. _____. "In-house Procedures in a Library using Codoc." *Government Publications Review* 8A (1981): 413-18.

11. _____, and Presser, Carolynne. "Codoc—A Quick, Inexpensive, Computer-based System for Handling Government Documents." Paper presented at the 1977 Conference of the Western Canadian Chapter of the American Society for Information Science (ASIS).

12. Grenier, Patricia. "Codoc—A Computer-Based System for Processing and Retrieving Documents." Paper presented at the North American Preparatory Seminar for the 2nd International Symposium on Documentation of the United Nations and other Intergovernmental Organizations (International Documents— New Directions.) June 20-22, 1979.

13. Hajnal, Peter; de Bruin, Valentina; and Biteen, Dale. "Marc and Codoc: A Case Study in Dual Format Use in a University Library." *Journal of Library Automation* 10 (1977): 358-73.

14. Hannah, Kerry. "Codoc for a Public Library." *Canadian Library Journal* 39 (1982): 79-81.

15. Knowles, Caroline M., and Pearson, Ellen M. "The Documentation Centre of the University of Guelph Library: Its Functions and Position within the Library Organization." *Government Publications Review* 1 (1974): 241-50.

16. Nyren, Karl, ed. "Buying New Technology." *Library Journal Special Report No. 4*. New York: R. R. Bowker, 1978.

17. Pearson, Ellen. "Codoc—A Co-operative Approach to Managing Government Publications." *Expression* 1 (1977): 18-22, 58-59.

18. _____, and Gillham, Virginia. "CODOC—Bibliographic Control of Official Publications." In *Bibliographic Control of Official Publications*. Edited by John Pemberton. Oxford: Pergamon Press, 1982.

19. _____, and Hrabi, Merv. "Guelph Document System." In *Automated Cataloguing Systems at the University of Guelph Library.* The LARC Association Computerized Cataloguing Systems Series, Vol. 1, No. 1, 1973.

20. Presser, Carolynne. "Codoc, Co-operative Government Documents, a Computer-based Processing and Retrieval System." *College and Research Libraries* 39 (1978): 94–98.

21. _____. "Organization of a Separate Government Documents Collection, University of Waterloo—A Case History." *Government Publications Review* 2 (1975): 167–76.

22. Ready, William, and Westell, Mary. "Codoc: A Canadian Cooperative Computerized Scheme for Published Government Documents." *Canadian Journal of Information Science* 3 (1979): 176–80.

23. Sadek, Nancy. "Codoc for an Archive." *Canadian Library Journal* 39 (1982): 75–78.

BIBLIOGRAPHY

Articles

Akoka, J. "A Framework for Decision Support Systems Evaluation." *Information and Management* 4 (1981): 133–41.

Beckman, Margaret. "A Documentation Centre at the University of Guelph Library." *Ontario Library Review* 50 (1966): 226–29.

"Cameras in the Courts." *The News Media and the Law* 5 (October–November 1981): 64.

Dula, Richard O., and Gaschnig, John G. "Knowledge-Based Expert Systems Come of Age." *Byte* 6 (September 1981): 238–81.

Flanders, Bruce L. "State Documents in Kansas Automated Bibliographic Control." *Documents to the People* 8 (May 1980): 114.

Ford, Barbara, and Nakata, Yuri. "Reference Use of State Government Information in Academic Libraries." *Government Publications Review*, in press.

"FNE Operates as Private Videotex System." *Today* (July/August 1982): 14–15.

Futano, Linda. "Online Bibliographic Database Searching for Government Documents Collections." *Government Publications Review* 9 (1982): 311–22.

Gillham, Virginia. "Codoc as a Consortium Tool." *Government Publications Review* 9 (1982): 45–53.

_____. "The Guelph Document System." *Government Publications Review* 7 (1980): 211–16.

_____. "In-House Procedures in a Library Using Codoc." *Government Publications Review* 8A (1981): 413–18.

"Guidelines for Microfiche Conversion." *Documents to the People* 9 (September 1981): 218–20.

Hajnal, Peter; de Bruin, Valentina; and Biteen, Dale. "Marc and Codoc: A Case Study in Dual Format Use in a University Library." *Journal of Library Automation* 10 (1977): 358–73.

Hannah, Kerry. "Codoc for a Public Library." *Canadian Library Journal* 39 (1982): 79–81.

Heindel, A. J., and Napier, H. A. "Decision Support Systems in Libraries." *Special Libraries* 72 (1981): 319–27.

Hernon, Peter. "Documents Librarianship in the 1980s: Current Issues and Trends in Research." *Government Publications Review* 9 (1982): 99–120.

Hunt, Deborah S. "Accessing Federal Government Documents Online." *Database* 6 (1982): 10–17.

Jones, Kathryn. "Lack of Net Standards Scored." *MIS Week* 3 (December 8, 1982): 25.

Knowles, Caroline M., and Pearson, Ellen M. "The Documentation Centre of the University of Guelph Library: Its Functions and Position within the Library Organization." *Government Publications Review* 1 (1974): 241–50.

Lane, Margaret T. "Scattered Notes on State Publications." *Documents to the People* 9 (September 1981): 186.

McClure, Charles R. "An Integrated Approach to Government Publication Collection Development." *Government Publications Review* 8A (1981): 5–15.

_____. "Microformatted Government Publications: Space and Facilities." *Government Publications Review* 6 (1979): 405–12.

_____. "Online Government Documents Data Base Searching and the Use of Microfiche Documents Online by Academic and Public Depository Librarians." *Microform Review* 10 (Fall 1981): 245–59.

_____. "Planning for Library Services: Lessons and Opportunities." *Journal of Library Administration* 2 (1982): 7–28.

_____. "Technology in Government Documents Collections: Current Status, Impacts, and Prospects." *Government Publications Review* 9 (1982): 255–76.

Morton, Bruce. "Implementing an Automated Shelflist for a Selective Depository Collection: Implications for Collection Management and Public Access." *Government Publications Review* 9 (1982): 323–44.

_____. "An Items Record Management System: First Step in the Automation of Collection Development in Selective GPO Depository Libraries." *Government Publications Review* 8A (1981): 185–96.

_____. "New Management Problems for the Documents Librarian: Government Microfiche Publications." *Microform Review* 11 (Fall 1982): 254–58.

_____. "Toward a Comprehensive Collection Development Policy for Partial U.S. Depository Libraries." *Government Publications Review* 7A (1980): 41–46.

_____, and Cox, J. Randolph. "Cooperative Collection Development between Selective U.S. Depository Libraries." *Government Publications Review* 9 (1982): 221–29.

Nakata, Yuri, and Kopec, Karen. "State and Local Government Publications." *Drexel Library Quarterly* 16 (October 1980): 40–59.

Pearson, Ellen. "Codoc: A Co-operative Approach to Managing Government Publications." *Expression* 1 (1977): 18–22, 58–59.

Phillips, Roger. "A Public Access Videotex Library Service." *Online* 6 (September 1982): 34–37.

Presser, Carolynne. "Codoc, Co-operative Government Documents: A Computer-Based Processing and Retrieval System." *College and Research Libraries* 39 (1978): 94–98.

———. "Organization of a Separate Government Documents Collection, University of Waterloo—A Case History." *Government Publications Review* 2 (1975): 167–76.

Purcell, Gary. "Reference Use of State Government Publications in Public Libraries." *Government Publications Review*, in press.

Ready, William, Mary West et al. "Codoc: A Canadian Cooperative Computerized Scheme for Published Government Documents." *Canadian Journal of Information Science* 3 (1979): 176–80.

Richardson, John V.; Frisch, Dennis C. W.; and Hall, Catherine M. "Bibliographic Organization of U.S. Federal Depository Collections." *Government Publications Review* 7 (1980): 463–80.

Roizen, Joseph. "Teletext: A Service That's Coming of Age." *Educational and Industrial Television* 14 (September 1982): 39.

"S&LDTF Business Meeting." *Documents to the People* 10 (May 1982): 111–12.

Sadek, Nancy. "Codoc for an Archive." *Canadian Library Journal* 39 (1982): 75–78.

Salmon, Stephen R. "User Resistance to Microforms in the Research Library." *Microform Review* 3 (July 1974): 194–99.

Shaw, Anne. "GODORT Microform Survey." *Documents to the People* 6 (January 1978): 27–28.

"State Governments Take on New Vigor." *U.S. News and World Report* (March 20, 1978): 39–40, 42–43.

Swanson, Don R. "Miracles, Microcomputers, and Librarians." *Library Journal* 107 (June 1, 1982): 1055–59.

Tepfer, Charles S. "Keeping up with Videotext." *Educational and Industrial Television* 14 (September 1982): 36.

Urrows, Henry and Elizabeth. "Can Videotext Work?" *Microcomputing* 5 (October 1981): 68.

VanCamp, Ann. "Effective Search Analysts." *Online* 3 (April 1979): 18–20.

Walbridge, Sharon. "OCLC and Government Documents Collections." *Government Publications Review* 9 (1982): 277–87.

Weiss, Henry. "Problem with Videotext: Still too Smart for Some Users." *MIS Week* (March 18, 1982): 26.

Books

Boomer, M.R., and Chorba, R.W. *Decision Making for Library Management*. White Plains, NY: Knowledge Industries, 1982.

Boss, Richard W. *The Library Manager's Guide to Automation*. White Plains, NY: Knowledge Industries, 1979.

Corbin, John. *Developing Computer Based Library Systems*. Phoenix, AR: Oryx Press, 1981.

Evans, Christopher. *The Micro Millenium*. New York: Washington Square Press, 1981.

Fisher, Mary L. *Guide to State Legislature Materials*. Littleton, CO: Rothman, 1979.

Hernon, Peter. *Communicating Public Access to Government Information*. Westport, CT: Meckler Publishing, 1983.

Hoover, Ryan E. *The Library and Information Manager's Guide to Online Services*. White Plains, NY: Knowledge Industries, 1980.

Kathman, Michael D., and Massman, Virgil F. *Options for the 80s: Proceedings of the Second National Conference of the Association of College and Research Libraries*. 2 vols. Greenwich, CT: JAI Press, 1982.

Library Data Collection Handbook. Chicago: American Library Association, 1981.

McClure, Charles R. *Information for Academic Library Decision Making: The Case for Organizational Information Management*. Westport, CT: Greenwood Press, 1980.

_____, and Hernon, Peter. *Improving the Quality of Reference Service for Government Publications*. Chicago: American Library Association, 1983.

McCorduck, Pamela. *Machines Who Think: A Personal Inquiry into the History and Prospects of Artificial Intelligence*. San Francisco: W.H. Freeman and Co., 1979.

Matthews, Joseph R. *Choosing an Automated Library System: A Planning Guide*. Chicago: American Library Association, 1980.

Michie, Donald. *Expert Systems in the Micro-electronic Age*. Edinburgh: Edinburgh University Press, 1979.

Myers, Darlene. *Computer Science Resources: A Guide to Professional Literature*. White Plains, NY: Knowledge Industries, 1981.

Nyren, Karl. *Buying New Technology*. Library Journal Special Report No. 4. New York: R. R. Bowker, 1978.

Sigel, Efrem. *Videotext: The Coming Revolution in Home/Office Information Retrieval*. White Plains, NY: Knowledge Industries, 1980.

Smith, Anthony. *Goodbye Gutenberg: The Newspaper Revolution of the 1980's*. New York: Oxford University Press, 1980.

U.S. Library of Congress. Science Policy Division. *State Legislative Use of Information Technology* (Reprint of House Document No. 95–271. 95th Congress, 1st Session, originally issued in 1977). Westport, CT: Greenwood Press, 1978.

Contributions to Books

Gorman, Michael. "The Prospective Catalog." In *Closing the Catalog: Proceedings of the 1978 and 1979 Library and Information Technology Associates Institutes*. Phoenix, AR: Oryx Press, 1980.

Halloran, Norbert A. "Computers in Court Administration." In *Computers and the Law*, edited by R.P. Bigelow, 3rd ed. Chicago: Commerce Clearing House, 1981.

Hartman, Ruth D. "Options for the 80s: How Does the Documents Librarian Meet the Challenges of the 80s?" In *Options for the 80s: Proceedings of the Second National Conference of the Association of College and Research Libraries*. Greenwich, CT: JAI Press, 1982.

Heim, Kathleen M. "Government Produced Machine-Readable Statistical Data as a Component of the Social Science Information System: An Examination of Federal Policy and Strategies for Access." In *Communicating Public Access to Government Information*, edited by Peter Hernon. Westport, CT: Meckler Publishing, 1982.

McClure, Charles R. "Management Information for Library Decision Making." In *Advances in Librarianship*, edited by W. Simonton, vol. 12. New York: Academic Press, 1983.

Pearson, Ellen and Gillham, Virginia. "CODOC: Bibliographic Control of Official Publications." In *Bibliographic Control of Official Publications*. Edited by John Pemberton. Oxford, England: Pergamon Press, 1982.

_____, and Hrabi, Merv. "Guelph Document System." In *Automated Cataloguing Systems at the University of Guelph Library*. In the LARC Association Computerized Cataloguing Systems Series, Vol. 1, No. 1, 1973.

Vorlander, Carl W. "State Information Systems." In *Book of the States, 1980–81*. Lexington, KY: Council of State Governments, 1980.

Government Publications (United States)

Case, Donald et al. *Standford Evaluation of the Green Thumb Box Experimental Video-text Project for Agricultural Extension Information Delivery in Shelby and Todd Counties, Kentucky*. Springfield, VA: National Technical Information Service, 1981 (PB 82-190281).

Depository Library Council to the Public Printer, Transcript of the Fall 1982 Meeting, 1982. (GP 3.30:982/2)

Depository Library Council to the Public Printer, Transcript of the Spring 1982 Meeting, 1982. (GP 3.30:982)

Domestic Council. Committee on the Right of Privacy. *National Information Policy: Report to the President of the United States*. Washington, DC: National Commission on Libraries and Information Science, 1977.

National Commission on Libraries and Information Science. *Public Sector/Private Sector Interaction in Providing Information Services*. Washington, DC: GPO, 1982.

Summary Report of Depository Libraries. Washington: GPO, October 1979.

Papers and Reports

Beckman, Margaret. *Documentation System for the Organization of Government Publications within a University Library*. Research Report No. 2. Guelph, Ontario: University of Guelph Library, 1969.

_____; Henderson, Sara; and Pearson, Ellen. *The Guelph Document System*. Report No. 3. Guelph, Ontario: University of Guelph Library, 1973.

_____, and Pearson, Ellen. *Co-operative Use of the Guelph Document System.* Guelph, Ontario: University of Guelph, 1974.

CODOC Coding Manual. Toronto, Canada: Office of Library Co-ordination, Council of Ontario Universities, May 1976.

Faull, Sandra. *The Codoc System at Stockton State College.* Unpublished paper. Pomona, NJ: Stockton State College Library, 1976.

Gillham, Virginia. "CODOC: A Canadian System for Processing Government Publications." Paper presented to the Official Publications section of I.F.L.A., Montreal, Canada, August 24, 1982.

_____, and Presser, Carolynne. "Codoc: A Quick, Inexpensive, Computer-Based System for Handling Government Documents." Paper presented at the 1977 Conference of the Western Canadian Chapter of the American Society for Information Science (ASIS).

Grenier, Patricia. "Codoc: A Computer Based System for Processing and Retrieving Documents." Paper presented at the North American Preparatory Seminar for the 2nd International Symposium on Documentation of the United Nations and Other Intergovernmental Organizations. (International Documents—New Directions.) June 20–22, 1979.

Winner, Ronald, and Kirk, Sherwood. "Illinois Document Depository Libraries Use of OCLC Cataloging for the Depository Collection: A Survey with Implications for Revision of the Depository Program." Mimeographed. Springfield, IL: Illinois State Library, 1981.

CONTRIBUTORS

PETER HERNON, who received his Ph.D. degree from Indiana University, Bloomington, is Associate Professor at the Graduate School of Library and Information Science, Simmons College, Boston. His teaching and research interests relate to government publications, reflective inquiry and research methods, reference services, and the social sciences. He has written extensively in the documents field, particularly on topics relating to reference services, collection development, the GPO depository library program, and use of government publications. Two of his books include *Use of Government Publications by Social Scientists* (1979) and *Developing Collections of U.S. Government Publications* (1982). He is currently working on a textbook on government publications that examines the critical issues of public access and collection development across levels of government. Co-authored with Charles R. McClure, this book will be published in the spring of 1984 by Ablex Publishing Corporation, Norwood, New Jersey.

VIRGINIA GILLHAM has served as Head of the Documentation and Media Resource Centre, University of Guelph, since 1975. Prior to assuming this position, she was Head of Circulation (1973–1975) and Reserve Librarian (1972–1973) at the University. She has also been Catalogue Librarian, University of Northern Colorado at Greeley (1970–1972). Ms. Gillham received her B.A. degree from McMaster

University, Hamilton, Ontario, and her M.S.L.S. from the University of Illinois, Urbana. She has authored several articles on the CODOC system and served as Executive Member of the CODOC User Group (1976–1978). Since 1978 she has served as the chair of the Group. She is also a National Level Judge, Canadian Figure Skating Association.

CHARLES R. McCLURE is Associate Professor at the School of Library Science, University of Oklahoma, and received his Ph.D. degree from Rutgers University in Library and Information Services in 1977. He has served as Head of the Government Documents Department at the University of Texas at El Paso Library. Currently, he teaches in the areas of government publications, library administration, systems analysis, and the planning and evaluation of library services.

He has served as Assistant Editor of *Government Publications Review* and has written a regular column, "Microformatted Government Publications," for that publication. McClure has published a number of articles related to administration and government documents, the most recent being "Technology in Government Document Collections," in a special issue of *Government Publications Review*. His monographs include *Information for Academic Library Decision Making: The Case for Organizational Information Management* (Greenwood Press, 1980) and *Planning for Library Services* (Haworth Press, 1982). He is also co-author, with Peter Hernon, of *Improving the Quality of Reference Service for Government Publications* (American Library Association, 1983).

BRUCE MORTON is Associate Librarian, Information Services and Government Documents, at Carleton College, Northfield, Minnesota. He received his B.A. and M.A. degrees in English from the Pennsylvania State University and his M.L.S. from the State University of New York at Geneseo. From 1981 to 1983 he served as Coordinator of the Machine-Readable Government Information Task Force of the American Library Association's Government Documents Round Table (GODORT). He has published articles in *Government Publication Review*, *Microform Review*, *Minnesota Libraries*, *Reference Services Review*, *Technicalities*, *Improving College and University Teaching*, and various other journals.

JUDY MYERS, Documents Librarian at the University of Houston, Central Campus, received her B.S. and M.L.S. degrees from Louisiana State University. She is interested in improving user access to documents, and believes that documents cannot be fully utilized in most libraries until records of them appear in library catalogs. She has therefore worked to improve the quality and quantity of the catalog records of documents, specifically at the UH library. Ms. Myers is a past chair of the Federal Documents Task Force of the American Library Association's Government Documents Round Table (GODORT), and also of the Documents Round Table of the Texas Library Association. She is a past member and chair of the Depository Library Council to the Public Printer.

SUSANNA SCHWEIZER, Assistant Professor at the Graduate School of Library and Information Science, Simmons College, Boston, teaches and researches in the areas of information science, information technology, library computer systems, online databases, operations research in libraries, reference services, and systems analysis in information services. Ms. Schweizer, who is a Ph.D. Candidate at the University of Pittsburgh, received an M.L.I.S. degree from that University in 1978, an M.S. (L.S.) from Columbia University in 1973, and a B.A. (history) from the State University of New York in 1971. She worked at the Yonkers Public Library from 1971 to 1975 and is joint author of *Online Bibliographic Searching* (Neal-Schuman, 1981) and *A Directory of Automated Systems for Career Planning and Placement Offices* (1979). She is also chairperson elect of the New England Online Users Group and a member of the American Society for Information Science (ASIS).

TERRY L. WEECH holds the position of Associate Professor and coordinator of Advanced Studies at the Graduate School of Library and Information Science, University of Illinois, Urbana. Born in Galesburg, Illinois, in 1937, he received his A.B. degree from Knox College in 1959; his M.S. from the University of Illinois in 1965; and his Ph.D. from the University of Illinois in 1972. From 1973 to 1976, he was Head of the Department of Library Science at Mississippi University for Women in Columbus, Mississippi. From 1976 to 1980 he was a member of the faculty at the School of Library Science, University of Iowa, Iowa City. His publications include "Evaluation of Adult Reference Service," *Library Trends* 22 (January 1974): 315–335; "Attitudes of School and Public Librarians toward Combined Facilities," *Public Library Quarterly* 1 (Spring 1979): 51–67; "Public Library Standards and Rural Library Services," *Library Trends* 28 (Spring 1980): 599–617; "Collection Development and State Publications," *Government Publications Review* 8A (1981): 47–58; and "State Government Publications in Microform," in *Microforms and Government Publications*, edited by Peter Hernon (Westport, CT: Microform Review, Inc., 1981).